THE FOOD SNOB'S
DICTIONARY

Also by David Kamp

The United States of Arugula

The Film Snob's Dictionary—with Lawrence Levi

The Rock Snob's Dictionary—with Steven Daly

THE FOOD SNOB'S DICTIONARY

AN ESSENTIAL LEXICON OF
GASTRONOMICAL KNOWLEDGE

Food Snob *n:* reference term for the sort of food
obsessive for whom the actual joy of eating
and cooking is but a side dish to
the accumulation of arcane knowledge
about these subjects

David Kamp
and Marion Rosenfeld

Illustrated by Ross MacDonald

BROADWAY BOOKS   NEW YORK

PUBLISHED BY BROADWAY BOOKS

Copyright © 2007 by David Kamp

All Rights Reserved

Published in the United States by Broadway Books, an imprint of
The Doubleday Broadway Publishing Group, a division of
Random House, Inc., New York.
www.broadwaybooks.com

BROADWAY BOOKS and its logo, a letter B bisected on the diagonal,
are trademarks of Random House, Inc.

Portions of the material published herein previously appeared in *Vanity Fair.*

Book design by Ellen Cipriano

Library of Congress Cataloging-in-Publication Data

Kamp, David.
The food snob's dictionary : an essential lexicon of gastronomical knowledge :
food snob *n :* reference term for the sort of food obsessive for whom the actual
joy of eating and cooking is but a side dish to the accumulation of arcane
knowledge about these subjects / David Kamp and Marion Rosenfeld ;
illustrated by Ross MacDonald.
p. cm.
1. Cookery—Dictionaries. 2. Gastronomy—Dictionaries. I. Rosenfeld,
Marion. II. Title.

TX349.K25 2007
641.503—dc22
2007003610

ISBN 978-0-7679-2691-1

PRINTED IN THE UNITED STATES OF AMERICA

5   7   9   10   8   6   4

Contents

Acknowledgments

The authors wish to thank Aimée Bell, Thomas Jones, Graydon Carter, Dana Brown, Norman and Lee Rosenfeld, Peter Kaminsky, Adam Platt, Clark Wolf, David Lynch, Josh Sens, Joan Feeney, Rob Kaufelt, Nina Planck, Charles Conrad, Jenna Thompson, Steve Rubin, Suzanne Gluck, Georgia Cool, and the merchants of the Ferry Building Marketplace in San Francisco and the Greenmarket in New York's Union Square. May your peaches be strictly seasonal, and your *jamon* always *Ibérico*.

An Introductory Note
by the Authors

Part groupie, part aesthete, part stark raving loon, the Food Snob is someone who has taken the amateur epicure's admirable zeal for eating and cooking well to hollandaise-curdling extremes. He wears Bastad chef's clogs even though he works in publishing or property law. He owns an $8,000 gas range with six burners and a griddle. He's collected the cookbooks not only of James Beard's first-tier protégés, Marion Cunningham and Barbara Kafka, but also of the all-but-forgotten second-tierers John Clancy, Felipe Rojas-Lombardi, and Maurice Moore-Betty. He makes his own stocks, has taken a night course in mycology so that he may forage his own mushrooms, casually alludes to the "sugar work" he performed in the course of whipping up his famous homemade Christmas confectionery, and bakes rustic sourdough loaves daily from the *pain au levain* starter he's had going since 1996.

In other words, he has gone to great lengths to

distinguish himself from *you,* the mere food enthusiast, for whom watching Giada De Laurentiis on TV and cooking Mark Bittman's "Basic Pot Roast" are kinda fun. Whereas you favor potatoes and onions, he traffics in celeriac and garlic scapes. Whereas you're keen on Granny Smiths, he insists that you haven't even *tasted* an apple until you've sampled a Newtown Pippin. Whereas you regard your outdoor gas grill as just wonderful, he grills only with fruitwoods and mesquite, brushing the coals with moistened grapevine cuttings when available. He considers Elizabeth David, Richard Olney, and Fernand Point his greatest influences, in particular the latter's masterful *Ma Gastronomie,* in the original French, which—*What's that? You don't know who these people are? Then . . . then shame on you!*

The Food Snob's Dictionary has been developed to function as both a defensive aid in dealing with such a person *and* as a primer for aspiring Snobs who wish to lord their knowledge over others. In either case, it will help you keep romesco straight from romanesco, which, on rough days, is difficult even for chefs.

Theoretically, the Food Snob's body of knowledge should be vast, bordering on infinite. Human beings have been cooking and eating since time immemorial, which means that the Food Snob should have much more turf to cover and act smug about than, say, the Rock Snob or the Film Snob, whose chosen fields of specialized orneriness have relatively short histories, measurable in decades.* But the good news is that Food Snobbery in its modern form is a relatively recent pathology, with a very manageable history and vocabulary. Only academics and kooks need concern themselves with ancient flatbread preparations and how the Byzantines manufactured the fermented-fish condiment known as garum. For the rest of us, this book will do.

A Brief History of Modern Food Snobbery

In the United States, Food Snobbery as we know it dates only to the period after World War II, when GIs returned to America besotted with French culture, and Americans visiting France as tourists found a populace that, in gratitude for the war effort, restrained its urge to condescend to its guests, instead graciously initiating them into the ways of its culinary riches.

Prior to that watershed moment, Americans were insufficiently curious about food to become Food Snobs. The Gilded Age produced a rash of robber barons who patronized the fanciest dining palaces in the big cities (such as Delmonico's in New York and

* For more information on Rock Snobs and Film Snobs, see, respectively, *The Rock Snob's Dictionary*, by David Kamp and Steven Daly, Broadway Books, 2005, and *The Film Snob's Dictionary*, by David Kamp with Lawrence Levi, Broadway Books, 2006.

Locke-Ober in Boston), but these gourmands were by nature vulgar and undiscriminating, pitchforking every variety of viand, oyster, langoustine, game bird, aquatic turtle, and sweetmeat down their gullets with scant consideration of the quality of what they were eating; for all but a few connoisseurs (see entry for BEEBE, LUCIUS, page 9), the sheer quantity and expense of what one ate were proof enough of one's social eminence.

But with the postwar emergence of a prosperous, Francophilic middle class in America, both fancy cooking and restaurant-going emerged as leisure activities. Julia Child's first flush of popularity in the early 1960s alerted Americans to the fact that it was possible, if one had thirty-six hours of one's life to set aside, to prepare at home a *Mousseline de poisson, Blanche Neige*—a molded fish mousse adorned with shellfish and covered with *sauce chaud-froid,* a gelatinous reduction of heavy cream, fish stock, and tarragon, applied in a succession of layers that had to chill and set before the next layer could be spooned on. Concurrently, an enterprising Californian named Chuck Williams was building up a kitchenwares empire called Williams-Sonoma in whose stores one could purchase copper colanders and specialized pastry molds without the inconvenience of hand-toting them from Paris and clearing them through customs. And Craig Claiborne began writing thoughtful, carefully evaluative restaurant reviews in the *New York Times,* read by millions, in which he actually mentioned the names of the chef and proprietor of the place he was critiquing. Crucially, he also assigned each restaurant a star rating, which was then a novelty.

For sane, well-adjusted people, these developments were embraced in a spirit of joy and good fun. But for a certain, less stable segment of the population, the starting gun had sounded on a new social competition: Who could be the Food-Snobbiest? In this group, it became a mark of status to know the difference between a *daube* and a *navarin* (the former is made with slow-cooked beef, the latter with slow-cooked lamb), to know how to prepare both dishes, and to know not only that "Craig" (the last name never uttered) had praised the *daube* at a Manhattan bistro called Le Poulailler, but that *le poulallier* means "the chicken coop," and that the bistro's owners were Robert Meyzen and Fred Decré, who also owned the more upscale restaurant La Caravelle, and who had previously worked at Le Pavillon, where their employer was Henri Soulé, who had made his name running the restaurant of the French Pavilion at the 1939–40 World's Fair and who had before that managed the Café de Paris in France, and who, as a young man, had waited on Escoffier, the founding father of classical French cuisine, unless, of course, you chose to bestow that honorific upon Carême, who worked for Talleyrand.

By the 1970s and '80s, Food Snobs had moved beyond France as their primary focus of interest. Paradoxically, this only made them snootier. Whether they were exulting in the superiority of Northern California's produce, baking hippie whole-grain health loaves, grinding their own coffee beans (Sulawesi, Sumatra, or Kona, depending on the hour of the day), or demonstrating that they had evolved beyond outmoded red-sauce perceptions of Italian cookery by making pesto and redoing their kitchens with Tuscan terra-cotta tile flooring, Food Snobs were broadening their repertoires, forever looking for new arenas in which to showboat. At the same time, food journalism became more conversational and knowing, with such magazine writers as Gael Greene (at *New York*) and Ruth Reichl (at *New West,* later called *California*) treating chefs like Hollywood per-sonalities—thereby arming Snobs with insiderist knowledge about food people ("Have you heard that Wolf is leaving Ma Maison to open a *pizza place*?") to complement their culinary learnedness. Newspa-pers, too, got in on the act, expanding their dining and cooking coverage from a page or two to a splashout weekly section—compulsory reading for any Snob worth his sea salt.

The 1990s saw Food Snobbery come under threat. Suddenly, in 1993, there was a TV network devoted entirely to food, and the ranks of celebrity chefs, once countable on two hands, grew to dozens, then hundreds. Fine food and serious chefs vaulted into the realm of popular culture, and what had once been carefully hoarded knowledge was now in the public domain. That coarse but promising young chef in New Orleans who had livened up the comatose Commander's Palace and then opened a fabulous New Wave Creole place in the Warehouse District? Now he was on TV, America's darling, joking with his house band and shouting "Bam!" That bearded, ponytailed smartass with the red hair who served remarkably creative Italian food in a tiny storefront Greenwich Village joint? There he was in a studio kitchen, hamming for the cameras in all his *molto*-ness as he rolled out pasta dough for orecchiette. Wolf Appliance, the venerable manufacturer of deluxe cooktops and ovens for professionals, moved into the consumer market, and compounded the pain this caused Snobs by merging in 2000 with Sub-Zero, the Wisconsin-based maker of fancy home fridges for rich dilettantes.

The Snob's proprietary grip on gastro-knowing-ness seemed to be loosening. And as the twentieth century turned into the twenty-first, this situation was only exacerbated by a climate newly hospitable to reality-television programs set in professional kitchens ("Fire two branzino and one monk! *Now!*") and salty, bestselling memoirs (e.g., Anthony Bourdain's *Kitchen Confidential* and Bill Buford's *Heat*) that clued in even noncommittal eaters to the juicy facts that a) kitchen staffs are rife with volatile drug users; and b) most actual cooking in fine-dining establishments is performed by undocumented Ecuadoreans and Mexicans. Was there anything left for a Food Snob to act snobby about?

Yet Snobs are nothing if not resilient, and the recent spate of foodist pop-culture offerings has only hardened their resolve to stay ahead of the pack. If it's a Sub-Zero that Joe Financier and his wife want for their new McMansion, then the Snob will purchase a restaurant-grade Traulsen refrigerator. If mere mortals are getting into making fresh pasta, the Snob will out-artisan them with a basement affinage cave for his homemade cheeses and a custom walk-in for the prosciuttos he's curing. You think you've got bragging rights because Chef Boulud gave you a tour of the kitchen at Daniel? Snob Dude has been to Ferran Adrià's *taller,* the laboratory workshop in Barcelona where the molecular gastronomist conjures new foods (fruit pastas, smoke-filled ravioli, pine cone mousse, talking ice cream, etc.) during the six-month-long off-season of his restaurant on the Costa Brava, El Bulli.

As in the days when Julia Child first electrified the nascent Snob community, sending its members clambering for *poêles* for browning meat and *mandolines* for slicing vegetables, the Snob sets himself apart from the pack by being a pretend professional. It is enough for an ordinary food enthusiast to master a simple zucchini quick bread and maybe a basic white loaf; the Snob must master the impossible croissant. It is enough for the casual reader to idly page through *Saveur* and *Food & Wine* at the doctor's office; the Snob spends hours dialoguing in the pretend-professional forums of Chowhound and eGullet. It is enough for an average home cook to take away a few simple principles from Thomas Keller's *The French Laundry Cookbook,* such as the importance of flash-blanching vegetables in a large pot of salty water at a rolling boil, then shocking them in an ice-water bath; the Snob must undertake the restaurant's foie gras torchon, which involves procuring a fine, raw, fattened duck or goose liver, soaking it in a milk bath for a day, butterflying and deveining it, marinating it in brine for another day, rolling it into a log, wrapping it in cheesecloth, poaching it in stock, and hanging it in the fridge for yet another day before serving.

It is often the case, in fact, that acute Food Snobbery is a prelude to a radical career shift into the professional kitchen. The editors of *The Food Snob's Dictionary* make no objection to those who wish to use this book as a preparatory guide for such purposes. Readers will have to look elsewhere, however, for checked pants and a cocaine supplier.

The Future of Food Snobbery

Food Snobbery finds itself at an interesting juncture at the time of this book's publication. The rise of food politics and the mainstreaming of organics, along with the related increase in public awareness of food sourcing and production methods, have added a moral dimension to what had previously been more or less a hedonistic pursuit. Food Snobs are no longer just *aceto balsamico* obsessives, radicchio growers, crêpe fryers, and truffle sniffers, but fair-traders, farm-to-tablers, and sustainable-istas; a vast wealth of new possibilities for righteous humorlessness has been created. Correspondingly, *The Food Snob's Dictionary* addresses the lingo of this new, symposium-friendly Snob Set. (See, for example, entries for COMPOST TEA, page 20, and HERITAGE TURKEY, page 51.) The editors have also paid heed to the parallel rises in primitivist and futuristic cooking methodology, examining, for example, both the importance of LIVE-FIRE GRILLING (see entry, page 62) and the vogue for *SOUS-VIDE* (see entry, page 98). Even so, the editors are aware that the food world moves faster than that of book publishing, and that new techniques, ingredients, and concepts emerge on almost a weekly basis. Such being the case, we promise to be joylessly vigilant in continuing to chart trends in sustainability and expensive kitchenware for future editions.*

Helpful Hints

Given the complexities and interconnections of the Snob universe, cross-references between entries are common and are spelled out in CAPITAL LETTERS for easy identification. The editors have also seen fit to identify certain entries with the Food Snob Vanguard icon 🧀 , which, given its reduced size, looks merely like a generic round of cheese with a wedge cut out of it, but is, in fact, a slightly runny hunk of Époisses de Bourgogne, the rich, extremely pungent French cow's-milk cheese that Brillat-Savarin himself (see entry on page 11) declared "the king of all cheeses." (And is best eaten, Snobs say, in its raw, unpasteurized state. Which you can't do legally in the United States.) In this book, the presence of the Époisses icon indicates an entry that is held in especially high regard by Food Snobs—for example, the English-born cookbook author and trailblazing Mediterranean pastoralist Elizabeth David, or the crucial descriptor *heirloom,* which, in a

---

* Readers are welcome to visit www.snobsite.com in order to keep pace with new Snob developments and aggravate the authors with complaints and purported glaring omissions.

mere two syllables, has verily recalibrated the way the Snob mind takes the measure of a tomato.

Finally, let us express our sincere hope that this brief volume serves not only as a handy reference but as a tool for understanding. Though they are sometimes impossible to live with and are wont to sharply order us out of the kitchen, Food Snobs are often our friends and loved ones. We must understand that theirs is a heavy burden to bear; uneasy lies the head that wears the imaginary toque. By letting them select the fingerlings at market, by indulging them as they geekily articulate their fantasies of someday meeting the food-chemistry guru Harold McGee and preparing a capon with him, we not only validate their passions but indulge the little bit of Food Snob in ourselves. For isn't it true, after all, that every one of us can admit to preferring artisanal bacon over Oscar Meyer?

THE FOOD SNOB'S
DICTIONARY

The Food Snob's Dictionary

A symbol indicates a Food Snob Vanguard item, denoting a person, an entity, or a concept held in particular esteem by Food Snobs.

Acme Bread Company. Gold standard of ARTI-SANAL breadbaking in the United States, based in Berkeley, California, and founded in 1983 by former CHEZ PANISSE busboy and house hunk Steve Sullivan, who was inspired to try his hand at baking while reading ELIZABETH DAVID's *English Bread and Yeast Cookery* during an overseas bike trip in his college years. Ferociously devoted to hand-formed loaves and organic ingredients, Acme has a lower profile than the corporate-artisanal brands it inspired, New York's Tom Cat Bakery and Los Angeles's La Brea

Bakery, but it enjoys a greater mystique, largely due to Sullivan's ponytailed, shamanistic presence and refusal to sell his wares much beyond the Bay Area. *Picked up an* Acme *herb slab at Monterey Market en route to the Orville Schell lecture.*

Adrià, Ferran. Spanish chef of appropriately surrealist, Dali-esque mien who functions as a lightning rod in the Food Snob debate over whether MOLECULAR GASTRONOMY is bracingly innovative or overwhelmed by gimmickry. The popularizer of the vegetable FOAMS that reviewers loved in Spain in 1998 but jadedly condemn in America now, Adrià, who operates out of a coastal Catalan resort called El Bulli (The Bulldog), combines a DayGlo aesthetic with a FERNAND POINT fealty to getting the most flavor out of his ingredients, resulting in such weird-

Ferran Adrià

ass but surprisingly edible creations as a sardine skeleton enshrouded in cotton candy and skinless green-pea raviolis that look like Dr. Seuss egg yolks. *I clocked some* Ferran Adrià *influence in those fruit soups that we sucked down from medical syringes.*

Affinage. The process whereby young cheese is refined and matured, usually in a cave or climate-controlled chamber. The anointed cheese-coddler, known as an *affineur,* rotates the cheese and beats, brushes, and/or washes it until it is *à point* and ready to be savored. In the latest manifestation of cheese-course mania, some American restaurateurs now employ their own *affineurs,* though no one has yet made the logical, inevitable step of marketing home affinage units in the vein of SUB-ZERO wine-storage units.

Ali-Bab. *Nom de foodie* of French gastronome Henri Babinski (1855–1931), a mining engineer who dabbled in cooking and published an epic volume called *Gastronomie Pratique, Etudes Culinaires* in France in 1907. The book, later translated and published in the United States in abbreviated form as *Encyclopedia of Practical Gastronomy,* is an unwieldy, floridly written melding of culinary history, ESCOFFIER-style recipes, and French-supremacist philosophizing ("As to Norwegian cuisine, it does not exist"), but it won Babinski a following that rivaled CURNONSKY's in his heyday. Ali-Bab is largely forgotten today, except by Food Snobs eager to demonstrate their familiarity with pre–JAMES BEARD authorities.

All-Clad. Pennsylvania-based cookware manufacturer whose signature stainless-steel pots and pans have long been coveted by Food Snobs for their durability, excellent heat conductivity, elongated "stay-cool" handles, and aesthetic appeal. The five-piece All-Clad starter set is a staple of wedding registries in such Snob strongholds as New York and San Francisco.

AOC. Abbreviation for *Appellation d'Origine Con-trôllée,* the strict, government-regulated classification system used in France since the 1930s to delimit the geographical origins of the country's more prestigious wines, cheeses, and olive oils, and the farming and production methods used to make them. Less than 40 percent of France's wines are considered worthy of AOC classification, a circumstance that has inspired an American vogue for using AOC as a status-redolent buzz-term, much like "Le" in the 1970s— for example, in 2002, the acclaimed Los Angeles chef Suzanne Goin opened an oenophilic small-plate restaurant called AOC. Analogous classifications in other countries include DOC (*Denominazione di Origin Controllata*) in Italy and DO (*Denominación de Origen*) in Spain.

Apicius, Marcus Gavius. Ancient Roman Food Snob, said to have been born in 25 BC. Though there were a variety of Roman gourmands of different eras who used the Apicius name, Marcus Gavius Apicius is the one credited with having written some of hu-mankind's earliest cookbooks. In *De Condituris,* de-voted to sauces, and *De Re Coquinaria,* a broader compliation of his recipes, Apicius functioned as a sort of first-century combo of LUCIUS BEEBE and FERRAN ADRIÀ, encouraging the subjects of Au-gustus and Tiberius to embrace the pleasures of fine dining, but also acting as provocateur by touting bonkers dishes containing nightingale's tongues and camel heels. Legend has it that Apicius, having exhausted his financial resources and therefore his ability to enjoy elaborate meals, opted to kill himself rather than eat pedestrian pleb food.

Artisanal. Adjective suggestive of handmade goods and old-fashioned craftsmanship. In the food world, a romantic epithet bestowed upon the cheesemaker, breadbaker, bacon-curer, etc., who labors in his or her integrity-steeped native locale, independent of the pressures and toxicities of Big Food, to produce exquisite high-end, SMALL-BATCH edibles available by mail-order. *The farmstand's shelves groaned with a dazzling array of* artisanal *pickles.*

Asian street food. Increasingly chic trope-inspiration among chefs and restaurateurs (e.g., Jean-Georges Vongerichten and Anthony Bourdain) who have eaten their way through Saigon, Rangoon, Singapore, Bangkok, and Jakarta, and have somehow decided that they have seen the future of all cuisine. *My new place will combine Viennese-bordello décor with a menu inspired by* Asian street food—*pho, satays, potstickers, all that shit.*

Autogrill. Overromanticized chain of rest stops along the Autostrada, the main highway system in Italy. Purported to offer the best sandwiches known to

Christendom, and on the roadside, no less, Autogrills have served as inspiration to such American haute-sandwich entrepreneurs as Tom Colicchio and Nancy Silverton. In actuality, while Autogrill espresso is reliably good, the food is often merely passable and the bread downright unpleasant, meaning that its American imitators "do" the Autogrill better than the Autogrill itself.

Bain-marie. Overwrought term for "double boiler," deployed especially by retailers trying to sell expensive, purpose-built double-pot sets to status-hungry home cooks, even though it's easy to improvise a bain-marie with garden-variety roasting and sauce pans. Oddly, the *marie* part of the term (*bain* is simply French for "bath") comes from an ancient alchemist known as Mary the Jewess, who believed that using a double boiler's indirect heat simulated the natural processes by which precious metals formed.

Bain-marie

Bánh mì. Cheap, hoagie-like Vietnamese sandwich that reflects that country's French-colonial influence, being a baguette segment sliced open and filled with pickled vegetables, salad greens, and usually a meaty filling (e.g., roasted pork, chicken, meatballs, or even pâté). Long an unremarkable if satisfying staple of ASIAN STREET FOOD, the bánh mì has recently emerged as a fetish object for Caucasian Sandwich Snobs, first on the West Coast, where Vietnamese immigrants popularized it, and then in the Northeast, where competitive food journalists trip over each other to declare this storefront's or that pushcart's as "the best damned bánh mì in the city."

Baum, Joe. Brash, cigar-chomping aphorist-restaurateur (1920–1998), beloved by restaurant professionals, unknown to laypeople, and therefore a god to

Snobs. Working first for the New York hospitality company Restaurant Associates and later on his own, Baum was adamant that fine dining in America didn't have to be toe-the-line French, a vision that he sometimes executed successfully (the Four Seasons, Windows on the World) and sometimes not (the Roman-themed Forum of the Twelve Caesars, featuring gladiator helmets as ice buckets, and the Newarker, a white-linen restaurant romantically set in . . . Newark Airport). A reliable quote machine for food journalists (e.g., "When in doubt, flambé"), Baum is often credited with/blamed for coining the word *foodie. The boob-like double pineapple upside-down cake with Medjool dates for nipples was vintage* Baum.

Beard, James. Buddha of twentieth-century American gastronomy (1903–1985), literally and figuratively casting a long shadow. From the 1940s onward, Beard, via cookbooks, newspaper columns, kitchen classes, TV appearances, and advertisements, charmed middle Americans into liking home-cooked food—an audaciously against-the-grain stance in the gelatin-salad era. Drawing heavily from a childhood spent at the foot of his Oregon innkeeper mother, Beard promulgated the cause of American food decades before the NEW AMERICAN movement, and was revered by contemporaneous Food Snobs for his uncommonly refined palate and acute knack for TASTE MEMORY. Tidy in public life, where he favored bow ties and tweed jackets (he tended toward boatnecked French sailor shirts and ornate Chinese robes in private), Beard was untidy in his personal life, presiding over a chaotic menagerie of feuding amanuenses, hangers-on, and ex-boyfriends in a Greenwich Village town house that later became the home of the similarly untidy (until recently) James Beard Foundation.

Beebe, Lucius. Poncey, immaculately turned-out American society writer and gourmand of the screwball-comedy era (1902–1966), best known for his florid *New York Herald Tribune* columns of the 1930s and '40s, in which he recounted his social adventures as a walker par excellence and his elaborate feasts at gouty Gilded Age–throwback hotel dining rooms. Though verbose to the point of lunacy ("The good life continues unabated in Hollywood even as in the days of hammered silver handset telephones and the first fine floodtide of early ordovician Goldwynisms"), Beebe was one of the first name writers to take fine dining seriously as a subject, earning him the grudging respect of Snobs.

Lucius Beebe

Berkshire pork. Upmarket pork from purebred swine of British pedigree, redder in flesh, more marbled in texture, and richer in flavor than standard, bland

American pork (which is justly described as "the other white meat"). In the nineteenth century, some Berkshire pigs were exported to Japan as a diplomatic gift from the Brits, resulting in the pork's popularity there under the name Kurobuta ("black pig"), a term unnecessarily bandied about by American butchers and restaurateurs looking for a WAGYU-like profit margin. *Everything on the menu tonight is outstanding, but I'd especially recommend the loin of* Berkshire pork *with chestnuts and apple-Calvados chutney.*

Biodynamics. Intense, holier-than-organic farming movement that essentially follows the precepts of SUSTAINABLE AGRICULTURE to the nth degree; the ethos of choice for Food Snobs who think that the organic movement has gone too corporate. Inspired by lectures delivered in the early twentieth century by education innovator Rudolf Steiner, Biodynamics is based on the concept of the farm as a self-sufficient, mixed-use organism dependent on the interrelations of the realms animal, mineral, and vegetable; unlike an organic farm, for example, a Biodynamic farm is *required* to have livestock with which the crops and soil can interract. A farm may be certified Biodynamic only by a mysterious organization called the Demeter Association.

Blumenthal, Heston. Yobbish-looking but floridly intellectual English practitioner of MOLECULAR

GASTRONOMY. Besotted with the works of HAROLD McGEE, Blumenthal, an untrained cook who opened a modest bistro called the Fat Duck in a Berkshire village in 1995, started fiddling with his food as his confidence grew, pairing white chocolate with caviar, fashioning a "sardine on toast" sorbet, and using a liquid-nitrogen bath to prepare a frozen green-tea quenelle with lime foam. Result: his first Michelin star in 1999, and three stars by 2004. Less resolutely molecular than the futurist FERRAN ADRIÀ and the self-serious Grant Achatz of Chicago, Blumenthal writes a column for the *Sunday Times* of England in which he provides tweaked, home-achievable recipes for such traditional dishes as spaghetti bolognese, fish and chips, and black forest cake.

Brillat-Savarin, Jean Anthelme. Worldly French lawyer-statesman (1755–1826) whose obsessive interest in eating well compelled him to write the Snob urtext *The Physiology of Taste,* a book that, in its fusing of recipes with personal memoir and witty gastronomical musings, anticipated by more than a century the works of M. F. K. FISHER (whose English translation of Brillat-Savarin's book is considered definitive). Brillat-Savarin is oft credited with the aphorism "You are what you eat," though what he actually wrote is the more socially trenchant "Tell me what you eat, and I shall tell you what you are." So revered is Brillat-Savarin in France that an especially vascular-plaque-generating Norman triple-crème cheese has been named after him.

Brining. The simple process of soaking meat for a prolonged period—hours to days—in a salty solution. Invented as a preserving method, brining has more recently become a popular flavoring method, often involving gussied-up solutions that include such ingredients as chilies, cloves, peppercorns, maple syrup, fruit juices, and beer. (The haute-sausage manufacturer Bruce Aidells coined the phrase "flavor brining" to describe this approach.) Brining is especially helpful for chicken and turkey, since the process not only saturates the bland white meat with flavor but adds moisture that prevents the breast from drying out. Snobs relish the challenge of finding a vessel large enough for a turkey to be immersed in, favoring reverse-chic buckets from hardware stores. *I'm brining a heritage turkey with some sugar and pickling spices to get that awesome deli-meat quality.*

Brown, Helen Evans. Early West Coast food authority (1904–1964) whose vigorous championing of SAND DABS, tortillas, and Dungeness crabs presaged the regionalist food booms of California and the Pacific Northwest, and whose voluminous, gossipy correspondence with JAMES BEARD, anthologized in a 1994 book called *Love and Kisses and a Halo of Truffles,* established her as a beloved, no-BS character in Food Snob lore. Her best-known work, *Helen Brown's West Coast Cook Book* (1952), not only includes history-steeped recipes for Lumber Camp Doughnuts and Portland Oyster Rabbit, but flashes of IRMA ROMBAUER–ish wit and innuendo, e.g., this passage on GEODUCKS: "Their necks . . . are such a grotesque sight that ladies of an earlier day stayed at a discreet distance when their men went hunting them."

Helen Evans Brown

Brunoise. Foremost of KNIFE SKILL challenges in the classic French repertory. An exacting yet basic preparation, used in garnishes and soups, a *brunoise* calls for an aromatic vegetable (e.g., carrot, leek, or celery stalk) to first be julienned, then precisely diced into tiny, uniform lengths, usually of no more than 2 mm apiece. Maniacal chefs are fond of dismissing unworthy brunoises as *"Sheet!"* or *"Merde!"* and then demanding that the cowed apprentice chopper start over.

Butter-poached lobster. Sumptuous lobster preparation popularized by THOMAS KELLER at the

French Laundry in the 1990s and since imitated, CRUDO-style, by restaurants across the land. The lobster is par-cooked, its meat removed from the shell, and then the meat is finished off in a pan, where it cooks slowly and gently in a water-butter emulsion, or *beurre monté,* resulting in an even richer dining experience and more suggestive MOUTH-FEEL than the normal boiled lobster with drawn butter. *The saffron risotto was topped off with a curled tail of* butter-poached lobster: *"Unnhh," groaned my blissful companion after her first bite.*

Cardoon. Vegetable of the thistle family, related to the artichoke, though treasured for its celery-like stalk. Long a staple of Italian cookery, the cardoon has gained popularity among Snobs for its versatility (it's good raw in salads or cooked in soups) and the frisson of pleasure one gets from saying its name.

Cardoon

Carême, Antonin. Social-climbing prettyboy French chef (1783–1833) who transcended his origins as a low-born pastry cook to become the greatest authority on French cuisine of the nineteenth century, concocting elaborate gorgefests for such clients as the French statesman Talleyrand and Alexander I, the czar of Russia. Though Carême is a necessary namecheck for any Snob who purports to know his culinary history, he is often cited in Snob discourse in unflattering counterpoint to French chefs of later eras. *The Troisgros brothers unabashedly embrace peasant fare; not for them the lofty pretensions of* Carême.

Antonin Carême

Celeriac. Confusingly named member of the celery family, grown not for its stalk but for its flavorful root. Often used interchangeably with the term *celery root,* especially by Snobs who enjoy perplexing nouns that sound like adjectives. Traditionally served in

Europe like a potato or turnip, in cooked and/or pureed form, though increasingly popular in the United States as a crunchy salad ingredient, served raw, peeled, and shredded.

Cèpe. Cloying French synonym for porcini mushroom, used on menus to confuse diners who think porcinis are old news. Truly pretentious chefs use the term *boletus* mushrooms for cèpes/porcinis, a shorthand allusion to the fungus's Latin name, *Boletus edulis*.

Chenel, Laura. Godmother of American goat-cheese movement. Starting out as a hippie back-to-the-lander in pre-affluence Sonoma County of the 1970s, Chenel, who professed to "belong to [her] goats," learned how to make chèvre in SMALL BATCHES, and in 1979 became the first commercial goat-cheese producer in the United States, with ALICE WATERS among her early paying customers. Chenel's chèvre operation, which she sold in 2006, grew to be America's largest in volume, though its cheese is not FARMSTEAD, given that the company purchases its milk from goat farmers.

Laura Chenel

Child, Julia. Enchanting, cormorant-voiced cookbook author and food-television pioneer (1912–2004), whose 1961 epic *Mastering the Art of*

French Cooking, Volume One (written with Simone Beck and Louisette Bertholle) and PBS TV program *The French Chef* triggered gourmet aspirations in ordinary Americans and professionalist pretensions in the burgeoning numbers of 1960s Food Snobs (as chronicled in a book specifically devoted to this subject, *My Kitchen Wars* by Betty Fussell). Belying the cute-old-lady persona assigned her late in life, Child was in fact a bawdy, fiercely liberal, whip-smart intellectual who partied harder than Anthony Bourdain. Snobs never use her surname, referring to her simply as Julia.

Chino Farm. Unassuming, smallish (45-acre) farm located just north of San Diego, known for growing produce so exquisitely flavorful that even diehard local-foods enthusiasts like ALICE WATERS resort to air-freighting it hundreds or thousands of miles to their kitchens. (Waters's Chez Panisse menus mysteriously refer to the farm as "Chino Ranch.") The farm's modest roadside stand, known as the Vegetable Shop, is a major pilgrimage site for hardcore strawberry oglers and those who wish to exult in the presence of the children of Japanese-American founders Junzo and Hatsuyo Chino. *I generally use only local stuff, but man, I fuckin' flipped when I opened up that crate of* Chino*'s albino beets.*

Chinois. Cone-shaped strainer with ultra-fine mesh or perforations; considered essential to serious chefs when making purer-than-pure stocks and fruit COULIS. The strainer gets its name, charmingly enough, from its resemblance to a Chinese coolie hat.

Chef ripped me a new one for the flecks in the consommé; I should have run it through the chinois *one more time.*

Chinois

Chioggia beet. Exuberantly food-stylist-friendly HEIRLOOM root vegetable. First introduced to America by Italian immigrants in the nineteenth century, Chioggias are a popular ingredient in $15 designer salads because of the concentric circles of red and white that they reveal when cut open, evoking Op Art and the Target logo.

Claiborne, Craig. Mississippi-born founding father of weekend-section food journalism (1920–2000). Cajoling his way into the running for food editor of the *New York Times* in 1957, back when newspaper food pages were considered a fluffy appeasement to the ladies and advertising gods, Claiborne won the job and proceeded to write serious-minded food stories and, as of the early sixties, restaurant reviews with star ratings, an innovation. Working in partnership with accomplished chef and HENRI SOULÉ protégé Pierre Franey on recipe columns, Claiborne flourished for two decades as the upper-middlebrow aspirational American gastronomist's Voice of God, overseeing *The New York Times Cookbook,* among other volumes, before spiraling downward into southern-gothic alcoholic despair and bitterness in his later years.

Coach Farm. Until its sale in 2007, the largest FARMSTEAD goat-cheese producer in the United States, located in upstate New York. Purchased in 1983 by Miles and Lillian Cahn, who were soon to divest themselves of their successful Coach leather-goods company (known for its handbags), Coach has become the East Coast's go-to brand of goat cheese, its aged peppercorn pyramid and super-rich triple-cream especially lauded by Cheese Snobs.

Cocoa nibs. Smashed-up, unsugared pieces of roasted, husked cocoa beans; ubiquitous as of the aughts as a dessert garnish and ingredient. Pastry Snobs, who consider gooey "death by chocolate"–style desserts to be oversweet atrocities for Disney World tourists, prefer cocoa nibs to chocolate chips as a texture enhancer in cookies and ice creams.

Commis. Polite French term for "galley slave." In the traditional ESCOFFIER-style kitchen hierarchy, each *chef de partie* (fish cook, pastry chef, etc.) had at least one commis to whom he assigned the most repetitive, unglamorous tasks of food preparation. This tradition continues in modern American kitchens, as does the hazing, burning, and abuse that drives apprentice cooks to alcoholism and drug abuse. *The* commis *did such a hacky job on the mushrooms that I just threw them into the stock and made the duxelles myself.*

Compost tea. Organic potion, heavily championed by the SUSTAINABLE AGRICULTURE crowd, that's made by adding water to compost, letting the mixture steep and ferment, and straining out the liquid, which is then sprayed on crops or poured into their soil. A well-made compost tea, which can use anything from molasses to fish scraps as a food source for beneficial microorganisms, works as both a pesticide substitute, keeping deadly plant diseases at bay, and as an enhancer of flavor and fertility for fruit and vegetable crops. *All it took was a few gallons of* compost tea, *and voila!—my orchards were free of apple scab.*

Concassé. French term for *coarsely chopped,* used on menus to describe an uncooked tomato sauce without sounding pedestrian. *The grilled dorade was perfectly complemented by a light, acidic tomato* concassé.

Cook's Illustrated. Avowedly uncommercial, subscription-only cooking monthly that offers unfussy, assiduously tested recipes and *Consumer Reports*–style evaluations of various kitchen implements and products. Cherished by Food Snobs who actually cook as a refreshing tonic to the advertiser-beholden glossy food monthlies (*Cook's Illustrated* pointedly accepts no ads and favors pen-and-ink illustrations over photography), the magazine's amiability and user-friendliness is undercut somewhat by the bizarre letters from its uptight, bowtied editor, the Vermont-based Christopher Kimball, who spins bonkers vignettes of his beloved flinty Yankee community, where he and his neighbors seem to hold the rest of America in contempt.

Coulis. A strained purée or cooked sauce of thin consistency. Though most coulis are associated with desserts (e.g., rhubarb-vanilla gelato with raspberry coulis), restive chefs are now making coulis out of everything they can think of, from uni (sea urchins) to CÈPES.

Country ham. Salty staple of southern gorging, at once championed by Heritage Snobs as an endangered piece of culinary Americana and fiercely guarded as a regional specialty that non-southerners have no business eating or trying to produce. Unlike most American hams, which are injected with water or brine and drip liquid when sliced, a country ham is dry-cured (with tons of salt and usually some sugar and saltpeter) and aged for months— or, in some cases, years—resulting

Country ham

in a forbidding outer crust of gray mold that must be trimmed off and a hard texture that warrants soaking the ham overnight before baking it. A Virginia variety of country ham, the Smithfield, is upheld as the ne plus ultra (and is produced and labeled according to strict, AOC-like legal statutes), though curers in Georgia, the Carolinas, and Kentucky beg to differ. *Mm-mm-mm, for Sunday dinnah, nuthin' beats Mama's buttermilk biscuits with thin slices of* country ham.

Covers. Professional term for "customers served," usually used as an indicator of how robust a restaurant's business is. *His Pan-Asian noodle joint is doing 480* covers *a night, but the quality has gone to shit and the money's going up his nose.*

Cowgirl Creamery. Womyn-tastic Northern California cheese producer and retailer, founded by two former Bay Area chefs, Sue Conley and Peggy Smith (the latter of whom spent seventeen years working for ALICE WATERS). Using organic milk from STRAUS FAMILY CREAMERY, Conley and Smith have fashioned a variety of ARTISANAL soft-ripened cheeses, one of which, the triple-cream, mushroomy Mt. Tam (named for California's Mount Tamalpais), has taken its place alongside HUMBOLDT FOG in the Cheese Snob pantheon. *Hurried into the* Cowgirl Creamery *shop in the Ferry Building for a quick wedge* *of Red Hawk, but they insisted that I wait for them to cut it to order.*

Crépinette. Small French sausage that confuses people who think that they have ordered a tiny crêpe. Crépinettes are made of minced, seasoned meat—often "variety" cuts like pig's feet and calf's brains—that has been wrapped in caul fat (*crépine* in French), which melts during cooking, adding a pleasing, unctuous MOUTHFEEL to the finished product.

Creuset, Le. Venerable French manufacturer of expensive enamel-covered cast-iron cookware that comes, incongruously but charmingly, in Cinco de Mayo colors. Most Snob wintertime cooking involves maneuvering very heavy Le Creuset casseroles and cocottes (oval-shaped Dutch ovens) around the kitchen, which are made even heavier by the joints of meat and root vegetables braising in them. *That nine-and-a-half-quart* Le Creuset *pot I got for my wedding still comes in handy on New Year's Day when the whole damned family comes over for Boeuf Bourguignon.*

Le Creuset

Crudo. Italian word for *raw,* repurposed by American chef-fisherman Dave Pasternack to denote the sampler of uncooked fresh fish he serves sashimi-style but with Italian condiments (olive oil, sea salt, etc.) at

Esca, his New York restaurant. The "crudo tasting" was such a sensation upon the restaurant's opening in 2000 that it was imitated by chefs across the country, much to the chagrin of cranky food critics, who saw it as an example of crass imitation rather than skilled homage.

CSA. Abbreviation for Community Supported Agriculture, a program in which members of a local community pre-pay a local farm operation for a share of its yield, ensuring that farmers get money up front to cover operating costs and living expenses in good years and bad. Like the related concept of SUSTAINABLE AGRICULTURE, CSAs are noble and admirable in mission yet often the province of mirthless, preachy people who like to make their fellow Americans feel valueless and shallow. *Did you know that* CSA *families are more likely to avoid divorce, live longer, do volunteer work, compost, and not have cable TV?*

Curnonsky. Pen name of Maurice Edmond Sailland (1872–1956), the premier French food writer of his time, known in Paris as the "prince of gastronomes." A sort of proto–JAMES BEARD, with his regal presence and hulking figure ("not dissimilar to an unfinished tub of butter"—Gertrude Stein), Curnonsky invented the concept

Curnonsky

of foodie-as-celebrity, referring to himself in the third person and causing gasps of thrilled recognition wherever he dined. Morbidly obese at the end of his life, he died when, one summer day, he leaned too far out a window, tipped over, and landed with a splat on the street below.

A PRONUNCIATION
GUIDE TO FOOD
SNOB–ESTEEMED
PERSONAGES

Grant ACK-etz: Grant Achatz, intense Chicago molecular gastronomist

Don-YELL Boo-LOO: Daniel Boulud, preeminent French chef-restaurateur in NYC

Wylie Dew-FRAYNE: Wylie Dufresne, mutton-chopped NYC chef-experimentalist

Larry FOR-gee-OH-nee: Larry Forgione, Americana-promoting chef, "inventor" of free-range chicken

Pierre Fruh-NAY: Pierre Franey, chef and long-time *New York Times* collaborator with Craig Claiborne

Suzanne GO-in: Suzanne Goin, Los Angeles wunderkind behind Lucques and AOC

Emeril La-GOSS-ee: Emeril Lagasse, New Orleans chef turned national brand

Zhock Pay-PANN: Jacques Pépin, cookbook and food-television eminence

Alfred Por-TAH-lay: Alfred Portale, influential chef and vertical food enthusiast, Gotham Bar and Grill, New York

Ruth RYE-shul: Ruth Reichl, *Gourmet* editor and serial memoirist

Eric Reh-PEAR: Eric Ripert, hunkish fish-finesser at Le Bernardin in New York

Ghee Sav-WAH: Guy Savoy, French big-timer now with an operation in Vegas

Eli ZAY-bar: Eli Zabar, ornery high-end food retailer

Tim and Nina Zuh-GATT: Tim and Nina Zagat, guidebook entrepreneurs

David, Elizabeth. Snob-exalted English food writer (1913–1992) and trailblazer of what Alexander Cockburn has called the "cookbook pastoral" voice. Taking an avid interest in Mediterranean and French country cooking in the postwar years, David turned out two masterworks, *Italian Food* (1954) and *French Provincial Cooking* (1960), which, though sometimes vague and imprecise in their recipes, neatly evoked a sun-dappled Southern European wonderland of LUSTY, un-gourmet-ish home cookery theretofore unknown to English-reading audiences. To Snobs, a far more important influence than JULIA CHILD (vis-à-vis French cookery) or MARCELLA HAZAN (vis-à-vis Italian cookery).

Dayboat. Menu qualifier for crabs, scallops, and, occasionally, finfish. More or less a synonym for "very fresh," the term not only emphasizes that the chef doesn't deal with farmed seafood or impersonal mega-suppliers but also conjures an image of a fisherman who awoke early this very morning, put on his slicker and Paddington hat, and returned by afternoon with his harvestings from the sea, which he bestowed upon the chef with salty good humor. The terms *diver* and *LINE-CAUGHT* are used to similar effect to describe, respectively, scallops and finfish.

Deglazing. Opaque chefspeak term for the simple process of adding liquid (usually wine, water, or stock) to a pan in which meat has been cooked, and then using a spatula or similar implement to pry loose the caramelized juices and bits of meat at the bottom of the pan, otherwise known—Snob bonus points!—as the fond. This fond-liquid mixture is returned to heat and reduced, becoming the basis for a sauce or a simple sauce in its own right. *I set aside the veal chop and* deglazed *the pan with some Barolo and the strained water I'd reserved from rehydrating the morels.*

De Groot, Roy Andries. Blind, unabashedly elitist British-born food writer (1910–1983) whose stand-out book, *The Auberge of the Flowering Hearth,* origi-nally published in 1973, detailed his obsession with a remote mountain inn, located in the Chartreuse re-gion of France, whose kindly old-woman keepers turned out impeccable plates of French country cooking. The auberge of the title quickly became overrun with upper-middle-class food tourists, set-ting a precedent for the Peter Mayle–driven sacking of Provence that occurred a decade and a half later. De Groot was also the first high-end writer to base a cookbook around the Cuisinart food processor.

Degustation. Highfalutin French word for a tasting menu, in which the diner cedes the process of choos-ing his food to the chef, who then sends out a succes-sion of small courses. Long a hallmark of fine dining in France, the degustation menu became popular in

America under the aegis of such chefs as THOMAS KELLER and Charlie Trotter, and has now migrated even to mid-level NEW AMERICAN restaurants. *For the month of August only, we're offering a five-course heirloom-tomato* degustation, *including Chef's unbelievable Yellow Brandywine sorbet!*

Dirty Girl Produce. Fruit and vegetable supplier whose wares, grown on a tiny farm in Santa Cruz, California, have been adjudged groovy by the Bay Area food mafia, and, therefore, by the greater Snob firmament. Founded in 1994 by two charismatic young surfer chicks, Ali Edwards and Jane Freedman, Dirty Girl is now owned and operated by a charismatic young surfer dude, Joe Schirmer. *I just* had *to make Portuguese soup; the* Dirty Girl *stand had all this gorgeous Lacinato kale.*

Dry-farmed. Adjective applied to fruit crops planted in spring, while the ground is still damp, and seldom, if ever, watered until maturation—forcing the plants' tap roots to seek out water from the earth rather than the sky, and resulting in fruits of vividly concentrated, rather than waterlogged, flavor. *You can keep your fancy heirloom tomatoes; me, I'm a* dry-farmed *Early Girl person.*

Ducasse, Alain. Streamlined, Bond-villain-ish French chef (born 1956) whose status as arguably the foremost culinary mind of his generation has been compromised by his brash forays into international entrepreneurialism. Making his name in the late 1980s at the Louis XV restaurant in the Hôtel de Paris in Monte Carlo, where his training under the NOUVELLE CUISINE stalwarts Michel Guérard and Gaston Lenôtre came to glorious fruition, Ducasse spent the nineties and aughts on an expansionist tear, opening multiple restaurants in France, Japan, and the United States. Though he is the only chef to have simultaneously rated three Michelin stars at restaurants in three different countries, his American efforts have suffered from a certain tin-eared, Mentos-commercial Euro-tacky sensibility that doesn't resonate with U.S. diners.

E. Dehillerin. Ancient, family-run cookware store in Paris's 1st Arrondissement; a mecca for American Food Snobs even though electronic shopping and the metastasization of Williams-Sonoma has undercut the uniqueness of the shop's inventory. *We couldn't help but make a pilgrimage to* E. Dehillerin, *scanning its overburdened shelves and racks in search of the copper-lined turbot kettle of our dreams.*

E. Dehillerin

Emulsion. Tricky-to-execute mixture of two unblendable liquids that must be achieved by slowly adding droplets of one liquid into another while vigorously stirring or whisking. Though emulsions have long been commonplace in cooking (in such forms as mayonnaise and hollandaise sauce), the word itself started appearing on menus only as of the 1980s, when show-offy chefs with fusion pretensions became fond of recklessly combining unorthodox ingredients. *Tuna tartare with daikon "chips" and yuzu–grapeseed oil emulsion, $26.95.*

Escoffier. Master French chef (1846–1935), who, though often cited as the source of the rich, severely codified French grande cuisine against which it's fashionable to rebel, was himself rebelling against the even richer, even more elaborate menus prescribed by CARÊME. Achieving worldwide fame in partnership with hotel manager extraordinaire César Ritz, Escoffier (whose first and middle names, George and Auguste, are seldom used by Snobs) articulated his vision of what is now seen as "classic" French cuisine in his book *La Guide Culinaire* (1903).

Escoffier

Expedite. Verb with different meaning in restaurant life than in real life (where it essentially means "to hurry along"). In a restaurant, an expediter is charged with the time-sensitive tasks of seeing that dishes are PLATED properly, getting a whole table's orders out simultaneously, and generally assuring that the kitchen is operating in sync with the FRONT-OF-THE-HOUSE staff. *Ever since Chef got his own TV show, he hardly ever cooks anymore; basically, he comes in two nights a week just to* expedite *and screams at us like a dick.*

Extra virgin olive oil. Oil that is extruded from olives in a single pressing, without the aid of chemical processes, and left unblended with lesser-grade olive oils. In Europe, there are strict AOC-style standards in place requiring that the oil have an acid content of 0.8 percent or less in order to qualify as extra virgin. Extra virgin olive oil has a fuller MOUTHFEEL and flavor than regular olive oil, and

Food Snobs consider it to be more of a condiment (for drizzling on raw vegetables or applying to a bollito misto) than a cooking ingredient, and warily regard any recipe that calls for extra virgin olive oil to be used in a heated pan.

Fair trade. Designation applied to imported food-stuffs whose producers, often ARTISANAL craftsmen or farmers of modest means, have been paid an appropriate wage and have been treated nicely by American buyers rather than exploited as the food-world equivalent of sweatshop labor. The "fair trade" designation is especially popular among groovy coffee retailers, who are conscious of the fact that their beans come from developing nations with suspect human-rights records, and who therefore assume that their affluent customers won't mind paying a premium for getting their caffeine buzz without underwriting the flaying of poor third world workers.

Family meal. Professional-kitchen term for the late-afternoon meal eaten by a restaurant's staff prior to dinner service; often abbreviated to "family" by hurried, harried workers. Though cobbled together from random scraps and leftovers, prepared by whomever is available (including dishwashers), and more intended as fuel than as delectable fare, the family meal has acquired a romance among outsider chef groupies and sycophantic journalists, particularly when prepared by Latino workers in a fancy restaurant. *Chef invited me to join in the* family meal, *a delicious pozole improvised from hominy, veal scraps, turnip tops, and slaw cabbage by Pablo, a playful, impish line cook from Jalisco.*

FAUX FOOD SNOBBERY

Six Foods That Non-Snobs Mistakenly
Believe Are Snobworthy (and That Snobs
Can't Be Bothered With)

Truffle oil. Most of it on the market is merely
overpriced vegetable oil augmented by synthetic
compounds that approximate truffle fragrance,
rather than fine olive oil infused with flavor
from actual truffle shavings.

Earl Grey tea. Maybe in 1972 it was still the
mark of a sophisticate to drink this black tea
perfumed with oil of bergamot, but now you
can get it in delis—with a "Lipton" tag on it.

Broccolini. This hybrid cross between broccoli
and Chinese kale seems exotic and greenmarket-
ish but is actually a supermarket-friendly Japanese concoction marketed by a Salinas Valley
agribusiness concern.

Kiwi fruit. This homely fruit—native to New Zealand and known as the Chinese gooseberry until an American exotic-produce supplier named Frieda Caplan astutely renamed it— symbolizes all the bad experimentation that went on in the name of nouvelle and California cuisine in the 1980s.

Chilean sea bass. For starters, it's not a sea bass, but a southern-hemisphere species more accu-rately known as the Patagonian Toothfish. What's more, it became such a hallmark of yup-scale menus and dinner parties at the turn of the twenty-first century (rather like Moby's album *Play*) that it was overfished, leading to regulatory crackdowns and a still-thriving black market.

Bell peppers in colors like orange and purple. Oh, please.

Farmstead. Lyrical adjective used to describe food-stuffs, usually cheeses, made onsite at the very farm where the dairy animals are kept and milked (or, in the case of farmstead baked goods and preserves, where the pertinent crops are grown). The ARTISANAL nature of farmstead cheeses, along with their elimination of a link in the FARM-TO-TABLE chain of production, has made them a cause célèbre in SLOW FOOD circles. *Alice welcomed us with a simple snack of* farmstead *cheddar, apple slices, and walnut-raisin bread. Perfect!*

Farm to table. Virtuous catchphrase for the movement to make eaters aware of precisely whom and where their food comes from—albeit only if this food is coming from local growers and ranchers who practice SUSTAINABLE AGRICULTURE. The apotheosis of the farm-to-table movement is Blue Hill at Stone Barns, a restaurant in New York's Hudson Valley situated on a working farm, obviating the need for fossil-fuel-consuming abominations like the horseless carriage. *We must find the shortest distance from* farm to table—*or perish!*

Fennel pollen. Exotic, pricey greenish-yellowish dust collected from wild fennel plants and used as a seasoning in modish restaurants, where its herbaceous funk is deployed to cut through the richness of such main courses as scallops and sweetbreads. *A* *mundane roast chicken turned into a sensual revelation after I sprinkled it with some* fennel pollen *I scored from my buddy's stash.*

Ferry Building Marketplace. One-stop San Francisco mecca for Food Snobs, collecting a wealth of Snob-approved alterna-brands—including FROG HOLLOW FARM, ACME BAKERY, SCHARFFEN BERGER, and COWGIRL CREAMERY—under one roof in the historical ferry terminal that abuts the Bay Bridge. Frequently confused/conflated with the Ferry Plaza Farmers Market, which operates four days a week just outside the building, featuring an array of vendors who practice SUSTAINABLE AGRICULTURE.

Ferry Building Marketplace

Field, Michael. Cautionary-tale food authority of the 1960s. Briefly as popular as JULIA CHILD and JAMES BEARD, Field, a wiry, self-styled "gourmet" who'd made his name as a concert pianist, excited aspirational bourgeois foodies with his cooking classes (initially run out of his home in Westchester County, New York) and his corresponding 1965 cookbook, *Michael Field's Cooking School.* Though a formidable enough figure to end up in JUDITH JONES's stable at Knopf, Field, tightly wound and prone to condescension, alienated most of the food world and died abruptly of a heart attack in 1971, when he was just fifty-six.

Fingerling potatoes. Amusingly gnarly and digit-like tubers that were early beneficiaries of the farmer's-market movement that took hold in the 1980s. Flavorful, available in many HEIRLOOM varieties, and better at holding their shape when cooked than standard Idaho varieties, fingerlings, by nature of their cute name and their natural side-of-the-plate compactness, are a popular secondary ingredient for florid menu-writers. *Tonight we have a special of line-caught sea bass, pan-seared and served with* fingerling potatoes *braised in wine until fork-tender.*

Fisher, M. F. K. Tough-broad Californian food writer (1908–1992) whose astringent, conversational essay collections, starting with 1937's *Serve It Forth* and continuing with such brilliantly titled volumes as *Consider the Oyster* and *The Gastronomical Me,* single-handedly rescued culinary writing from its chronic case of the twees—though, to this day, her admirers are moved to write appreciations of her that traffic in precisely the kind of cutesy gush she loathed. Snobs love referring to Fisher as "Mary Frances" (the *K* was for

M. F. K. Fisher

Kennedy, her maiden name), though very few were granted the privilege of calling her this to her face.

Flavor profile. Affected food-industry term for "how something tastes." Scientific analysts break down a food's flavor profile empirically rather than subjectively, determining its balance between sweetness, saltiness, sourness, and bitterness (and, if you believe in such things, UMAMI-ness), though food critics use the term more loosely. *Chef Phan's chicken claypot was a dazzling mélange of salt, heat, sweetness, and umami, very Southeast Asian in its* flavor profile.

Fleur de sel. Expensive French sea salt of labor-intensive provenance. Hand-gathered in the summertime by *paludiers* (artisan harvesters) in the Breton town of Guérande, fleur de sel is gently raked from only the top crust of the salt beds (traditionalists prefer female *paludiers,* who purportedly have a lighter hand), and the loosened crystals are bagged and sent to market. Snobs aver that fleur de sel is always to be used as a condiment, adding flavor and textural crunch to finished dishes, rather than as a seasoning in cookery, where it dissolves and its special qualities are lost. *I ate the purslane salad with just a pinch of* fleur de sel *and a drizzle of McEvoy Extra Virgin—the essence of simplicity.*

Flight. Term pinched from wine-tasting, denoting a sampler of a food in some of its different varieties. *I* *urge you to begin with our olive-oil* flight, *which features domestic, Spanish, Sicilian, and Israeli oils, and comes with crudités and ciabatta sticks for dipping.*

Foam. Sputum-like nuisance of the MOLECULAR GASTRONOMY era. Though the innocuous practice of frothing stuff up with egg whites is age-old, the 1990s saw such chefs as FERRAN ADRIÀ using laboratory-honed processes, such as blending a food with a gelling agent and then spraying it through a nitrous oxide canister, with just about any ingredient they felt like, be it mushrooms, asparagus, rhubarb, or foie gras. *His unorthodox huevos rancheros come with fried plantains adorned with chorizo* foam.

Foie. Professional-kitchen shorthand for foie gras (pronounced FWAH), necessarily uttered with off-hand cockiness. *What goes well with a blanc de blancs tasting? Easy! You just sear some* foie *and serve it with elderberry sauce.*

Forager. A person in the employ of one or more restaurants whose job is to scour the nearby countryside for wild edibles in their natural habitat, or, less romantically, to establish relationships with local specialty farmers who have cultivated esoteric produce. The very idea of the forager, redolent as it is of adorable woodland creatures scratching and snoofling their way across a pineneedly forest floor, is irresistible to Snobs, as are the names of such commonly foraged items as ramps, CARDOONS, and hen-of-the-woods mushrooms. *I first met my forager when she appeared at the kitchen back-door with a basket of the most gorgeous chanterelles I've ever seen.*

Forcemeat. Snicker-inducingly named standby of haute cuisine. A mixture of finely ground meat (beef, poultry, fish) held together by a binding agent (eggs, bread crumbs, etc.) and carefully seasoned, forcemeat can be used as a stuffing or as a dish in its own right, as when it's shaped into quenelles or a terrine. The quest to make perfect forcemeat was a central plot element of Michael Ruhlman's rhapsodic Snob-lit classic *The Soul of a Chef.*

Free-range chicken. Offhand menu colloquialism that, through frequent use, morphed into a de facto agricultural certification. While the chef of the River Café in Brooklyn in the early 1980s, Larry Forgione, hankering for the flavorful birds he remembered from his Italian grandmother's farm, partnered with an upstate farmer who allowed his chickens to roam the yards, unlike penned, pellet-fed commercial birds. Unsatisfied with the descriptors "natural" and "farm-fresh," Forgione concocted the adjective "free-range" to describe his birds' alternative chicken lifestyle. As such acolytes as JONATHAN WAX-

MAN turned to Forgione for sourcing, the free-range chicken took off as both a must-have item on NEW AMERICAN menus and a designation used by poultry farms—even though the USDA didn't and still doesn't sanction the term for official use.

Frog Hollow Farm. Deeply fetishized grower of organic STONE FRUIT, located in California's Sacramento River Delta. Founded by Berkeley native Al Courchesne, Frog Hollow won national renown when one of its peaches allegedly triggered ALICE WATERS's Edible Schoolyard project; as the story goes, Waters, biting into a succulent Frog Hollow "Cal Red," experienced an epiphany about the need for a curriculum that promotes gastronomical and ecological literacy in children. Frog Hollow has gone on to flourish as a brand name, with a line of preserves, pastries, and logo'd T-shirts.

Front of the house. Professional term for the non-kitchen part of a restaurant, encompassing the dining room, bar area, service stations, and welcoming area. The general Snob consensus is that the front of the house lags way behind the back of the house (aka the kitchen) at most American fine-dining restaurants, whose owners seek superior cooks but hire dim actors and models to serve the food. *Danny Meyer's hostesses and waiters are always friendly and tip-top; he's the only guy who gets* front of the house.

Garland. Venerable manufacturer of commercial kitchen ranges, grills, and ovens that, like the SUB-ZERO/WOLF company, has transitioned into making home products. Still, some Kitchen Snobs, in emulation of JULIA CHILD, who bought a restaurant-grade Model 182 Garland Range in 1956 (now on display at the Smithsonian Institution), insist on buying the company's commercial units, even though their heat output—up to 60,000 BTUs—is scarily hot unless a dedicated cooling and ventilation system is in place.

Garlic scapes. Curlicued, pinkie-width shoots nipped from hard-necked garlic plants early in the growing season, so as not to drain nutritional resources from the plants' bulbs. More often composted than eaten, garlic scapes have slowly emerged in recent years as a springtime greenmarket favorite in the vein of ramps and fiddleheads, as cherished for their ephemeral availability as for their mild yet still garlicky flavor, which works well in stir-frys and pasta dishes. *I was plumb confused when our CSA delivery included a mess of* garlic scapes, *but danged if they didn't make the loveliest pesto!*

Garlic scapes

Gastropub. Newfangled brand of restaurant, imported from Britain, that melds the splintery, beery conviviality of the English pub with the aspirational, seasonal cooking of the ALICE WATERS school, with the further enhancements of a poncey selection of wines and unbearable crowds. The Eagle, which opened in the Islington section of London in 1991, serving squash soup and rustic lamb sandwiches to young hipsters and bemused geezers, is widely credited as the first establishment to be designated a gastropub. The trend belatedly jumped the Atlantic in 2004, when Mario Batali and his partners opened the Spotted Pig in New York, and has since metastasized to such Food Snob–intensive cities as Seattle, Chicago, and Portland.

Gault-Millau. Shorthand term, pronounced GO Mee-YO, for *Le Guide Gault-Millau,* a French restaurant guidebook originally posited, at the time of its early 1970s birth, as a livelier, less snooty riposte to the entrenched *Guide Michelin.* Conceived by the youngish, severe NOUVELLE CUISINE champions Henri Gault and Christian Millau, the guide set out to shine a spotlight on the fresher, lighter, more inventive fare of younger chefs, but it has since ossified into an institution as implacable and anxiety-stoking as Michelin, a circumstance made painfully evident in 2003, when the star French chef Bernard Loiseau, allegedly distraught over a downgraded Gault-Millau rating, committed suicide.

Geoduck. Giant saltwater clam with alarmingly phallic siphon that hangs, John Holmes–like, out of its open shell. Especially abundant in Puget Sound, the geoduck (pronounced "gooey duck") is a mascot of Pacific Northwest foodie iconoclasm, as much a hallmark of Seattle's Pike Place Market as the mongers who throw salmon to amuse tourists. The geoduck is also a mainstay of Japanese gastronomy, where its siphon, thinly sliced, is treasured for its chewy, abalone-like texture and UMAMI-ish flavor.

Glace de viand. Thick, syrupy glaze used as the base for endless iterations of old-school ESCOFFIER-style sauces. Made by reducing and straining the heck out of a brown stock (usually of beef or veal, though *LAROUSSE GASTRONOMIQUE* includes an old recipe that incorporates "two dozen old hens" and "stag horn gratings"), *glace de viande* is an iron-man project that few modern home cooks are willing to endure; even Food Snobs sheepishly admit to buying it ready-made from an upmarket retailer.

Global knives. Very expensive, very fashionable, very sharp cutlery manufacturered in Japan. The subject of hot debate among Knife Snobs, Globals, distinguished by their design-forward dimpled-metal handles, are significantly thinner and lighter than those manufactured by the German standbys Wüsthof-Trident and Henckels, but are nevertheless regarded with suspicion by traditionalists who prefer European-style heft. *Ever since I got the* Global, *Chef has been more complimentary about my brunoises.*

Grass-fed beef. Beef from cattle who have been allowed to roam and graze in pastureland rather than mill about in pens, awash in their own filth and fed a species-inappropriate diet of grain and drugs; the rare menu qualifier (see also DAYBOAT and FARMSTEAD) that has actual nutritional import. The argument for grass-fed beef is that it's not only better for the welfare of the animals, who, as ruminants, are not equipped with the appropriate enzymes and bacteria to fully digest grain, but also better for human consumers, since the beef is lower in "bad" fats and higher in "good" fats than normal beef, *and* it's not loaded with the antibiotics that evil agribusiness ranchers shoot up their livestock with in order to overcome the liver abscesses the cattle develop from trying to digest grain.

Grass-fed beef

Hazan, Marcella. Stern, dry-witted advocate for Italian food in America, revered for her cookbooks *The Classic Italian Cook Book* (1973) and *More Classic Italian Cooking* (1978), and for disabusing Americans of the notion that Italian food was chiefly a function of Mob-movie histrionics and vast bowls of red sauce. A PhD in biology, she was a latecomer to cooking, turning to it only in the mid-1950s, when the career of her husband, Victor, required that the Hazans live in New York. Relying on her keen TASTE MEMORY, Hazan elegantly re-created the dishes of her Emilia-Romagna childhood, began giving cooking lessons, and was eventually discovered by CRAIG CLAIBORNE. Often posited as "the Italian JULIA CHILD," though the chain-smoking, no-nonsense Hazan willfully resists coming off as cuddly and is mildly peeved by the comparison.

Heat. Adjective increasingly vogueish among Food Snobs not in the traditional thermal sense but in relation to the palate-jolting, interruptive quality of chilies and horseradishes. Hardcore Snobs are fluent in the Scoville scale, developed by a man named Wilbur Scoville in 1912, which rates peppers from the heatless (sweet bell peppers) to the moderate (jalapenos and poblanos; both 4 on the scale) to the weaponry-grade (Scotch bonnets and habaneros, 9 to 10 on the scale). *The Scandinavian wintriness of the* *salmon tartare was offset by a delightfully unexpected kick of wasabi* heat.

Heatter, Maida. Patrician, white-haired doyenne of dessert-making, famously discovered by CRAIG CLAIBORNE when he came down to Miami to cover the food of the 1968 Republican Convention (Heatter's restaurateur husband, at her suggestion, was preparing elephant-meat omelets) and fell in love with her baking. Prone to endearingly barmy proclamations (such as that she can "hear" chocolate, which "sounds like a lover"), Heatter is among the most compulsorily readable of cookbook authors, especially when her recipes allude to her privileged upbringing, e.g., "When J. Edgar Hoover came to dinner at my parents' home . . ." and "If these aren't the same [macaroons] I had on the Riviera, I can't tell the difference." Frequently confused by Novice Snobs with Madhur Jaffrey, the Indian-born actress and cookbook author, who is nothing like her.

Heirloom. Term describing produce grown from non-hybridized, ages-old seed stock, which is often literally passed down from one generation of a farming family to the next. Like their furniture equivalents, heirloom fruits and vegetables are usually gnarled, fragile, idiosyncratically attractive, expensive when sold, and worth the money.

Henderson, Fergus. Poindexterish English chef known for his gutsy, ballsy embrace of guts and balls, among other "variety cuts" of cows and pigs. Since 1994, Henderson has promoted "nose-to-tail" dining at his restaurant St. John, located in the formerly grubby butchering district of London known as Smithfield. Propelled by the Cool Brittania wave of 1990s affluence and the macho boosterism of Anthony Bourdain, the unassuming Henderson has become internationally revered for such offal-centered recipes as bone marrow and parsley salad and crispy pigs' ears with sorrel. *Made the pilgrimage to St. John in London, where* Fergus *blew me away with a comped plate of duck's hearts on toast.*

Heritage turkey. Wattled-fowl equivalent of HEIRLOOM produce, denoting old-line indigenous breeds of turkeys that have approached extinction during the tyrannical, Butterball-fueled reign of the big-breasted hybrid freak known in the poultry industry as the Large White. Propelled by such organizations as SLOW FOOD, heritage turkeys, with such J. Crew–catalog names as Bourbon Red, Standard Bronze, Narragansett, and Jersey Buff, have been reintroduced in limited quantities to the market. *The* heritage turkey *we prepared for Thanksgiving was so dark-meated*

Heritage turkey

and intensely flavorful that Gramma wept as she said, "This! This is what turkeys tasted like in my girlhood in Vermont!"

Hildon. Posh brand of naturally filtered mineral water from the chalkhills of Hampshire, in southern England. Already a cult favorite for its crisp, unslimy MOUTHFEEL and high-aesthetic, blue-labeled, Anglophilia-stoking bottle, Hildon achieved greater recognition in the United States when THOMAS KELLER selected it as the official flat water of the French Laundry, where waiters tout it as "Thomas's favorite water."

Hob. British term for stovetop, seldom used in America except by Anglophile Snobs with ELIZA-BETH DAVID obsessions. *Oh, to have been there at No. 24 Halsey Street, aside Elizabeth as she loomed over her* hob!

Hudson Valley Foie Gras. Upstate New York pioneer in the U.S. manufacture of the traditionally French-made fattened-liver treat. Made not from goose livers but from those of the Moulard duck (a hybrid of the Muscovy and Pekin breeds), Hudson Valley Foie Gras, since its founding in 1989, has become a staple of re-gionally minded East Coast restaurants and posh food stores nationwide. *Next up on the tasting menu was a slab of seared* Hudson Valley Foie Gras *in a Concord-*

grape reduction, its membranous outside quickly giving way to a velvety ooze.

Huitlacoche. Earthy, love-it-or-hate-it Mexican delicacy, also known as corn smut, popularized in Southwestern and Cal-Mex restaurants by the buccaneering big-ego chefs of the late eighties. The sweet-corn equivalent of elephantiasis, huitlacoche is a fungus that attacks corn in damp conditions, dramatically bloating the kernels and turning them ashy-gray.

Humboldt Fog. Marvelously complex ARTISANAL goat cheese with a center layer of vegetable ash, produced by Cypress Grove, a Northern California company run by the earth-mama-ish Mary Keehn. At once accessible and rarified, Humboldt Fog is a common entry point for novice Cheese Snobs. *My perfect day would be spent on the porch during a lashing rainstorm with a bottle of Joe Phelps Insignia, a baguette from Acme, and a wheel of* Humboldt Fog.

Humboldt Fog

A GUIDE TO FOOD
SNOB NOMENCLATURE

How to Correctly Identify
Esteemed Food Personages in
Conversation with Other Food Snobs

"Simca," not "Simone" (for Simone Beck, Julia
Child's collaborator)

"J.G.," not "Jean-Georges" (for Jean-Georges
Vongerichten, internationalist chef)

"Jim," not "James" (for James Beard, food-
world paterfamilias)

"Biff," not "William" (for William Grimes, former *New York Times* restaurant critic)

"Tony," not "Anthony" (for Anthony Bourdain,
Kitchen Confidential author, TV host)

"Johnny," not "R.W." (for R. W. Apple Jr., late *New York Times* journalist and orotund expense-account gourmand)

"Wolf," not "Wolfgang" (for Wolfgang Puck, original celebrity chef)

"Doc," not "John" (for John Willoughby, grilling authority and *Gourmet* editor)

"Bud," not "Calvin" (for Calvin Trillin, author, humorist, part-time foodie-rhapsodist)

Induction cooker. Futuristic cooktop that, unlike traditional gas and electric ranges, uses electromagnetic energy to generate heat. Long popular in Europe and Asia but only a recent phenomenon in the United States (SUB-ZERO/WOLF rolled out its first American residential model in 2005), induction cookers offer a thermal controllability and specificity that old-style, inefficient ranges can't match, and also operate flamelessly, reducing the risk of embarrassing and painful "burner brands" on the hands. *My pulled-sugar hyacinths turned out amazing on the Bosch* induction cooker *I tried out during my stage in Brussels.*

Jamison Farm. Boutique purveyor of naturally raised lamb; the NIMAN RANCH of sheep-related products. Located in western Pennsylvania, the farm, presided over by the husband-and-wife team of John and Sukey Jamison, got its big break in the 1980s, when JEAN-LOUIS PALLADIN ordered three of its lambs for a congressional dinner, was enthralled to the point of tears, and spread the word among his fellow chefs.

Jamon Ibérico de Bellota. Deep-red, staggeringly expensive ham (selling for upward of $70 a pound) made from acorn-fed pigs raised on Spain's Iberian peninsula. Described by those who have tasted it as the orgasmic apotheosis of what pig-eating can entail, Jamon Ibérico has engendered an outright Snob frenzy with the news that the USDA has approved its import into the United States as of the middle of 2008—thereby making possible (at a steep price) an experience previously restricted to rich tourists on vacation in Spain and naughty U.S. chefs who've smuggled a ham or two through customs. In the reprehensible world of hedge-fund-underwritten Food Snobbery, people are paying three to four figures to reserve their own hams for 2008–09 delivery.

Jones, Judith. Francophile book editor of old New England stock, universally revered as the grande dame of cookbook editors (though she has also flourished as a "regular" editor, working with Anne Tyler and Sylvia Plath, among others, and commissioning the American publication of Anne Frank's diary). Presciently recognizing the value of JULIA CHILD and Co.'s *Mastering the Art of French Cooking* manuscript in 1960, after many publishing houses had passed on it, Jones urged her boss, Alfred A. Knopf, to buy and publish the book. For decades, Jones and her even more food-mad husband, Evan (1915–1996), author of such definitive works as *The World of Cheese,* presided over a New York intellectual salon that was like Lionel and Diana Trilling's but better, because it involved home-cooked meals and such guests as the Jones authors Child, JAMES BEARD, Jacques Pépin, and Madhur Jaffrey. *Don't get me wrong, I love working with Maria Guarnaschelli, but I wish I'd started writing cookbooks when* Judith Jones *was in her prime.*

Keller, Thomas. Intense culinary visionary and FERNAND POINT obsessive (born in 1955) whose primary outpost, the French Laundry in California's Napa Valley, is widely regarded as the best fine-dining restaurant in the United States. Relatively undecorated as a chef until purchasing and refurbishing the French Laundry in the early nineties (he was previously best known for his noble failure of a New York restaurant, Rakel), Keller pulled out all the stops, operating on a "law of diminishing returns" philosophy that the pleasure of eating any dish dissipates after three or four bites—meaning that a great meal should consist of many small courses. Tall, lean, and—unlike other famous chefs—distinctly unhammy, Keller carries a mystique that has inspired bouts of we-are-not-worthy genuflection by food writers, though his genial FRONT OF THE HOUSE and eccentric bill of fare (e.g., a "mac and cheese" of BUTTER-POACHED LOBSTER and mascarpone-slicked orzo) convey a great deal more humor and warmth than that of ALICE WATERS's Chez Panisse.

KitchenAid stand mixer. Bulbous, heavyweight counter appliance coveted by Snobs for its appealingly retro appearance and industrial-strength mixing abilities. Manufactured since World

KitchenAid stand mixer

War I, the KitchenAid is ideal for dough-kneading and even meat-grinding (with the appropriate attachment). Still, its sheer power and bulkiness can be intimidating to newlywed gift recipients, for whom the mixer all too often becomes an attractive dust magnet.

Kitchen Arts & Letters. Esoterically stocked, culinarily themed New York bookstore that, while so regularly invoked by reverent Snobs that it seems to be an ancient institution, was founded only in 1983. Frequented by actual chefs, serious journalists, and food-obscura enthusiasts eager to converse with the store's rumpled, Jewish Santa-like owner, Nach Waxman.

Knife skills. Machismo-measuring, phallically weighted index of a cook's worthiness, especially in a professional kitchen. *Dude can talk all he wants about his knack for combining weird flavors, but he ain't gonna get nowhere with those shit* knife skills.

Larousse Gastronomique. The gold standard of culinary encyclopedias. Originally issued in 1938 with a posthumously published foreword by ESCOFFIER, the book is composed of brief entries about specific foods, restaurants, notable culinary figures, and cookware, along with recipes pertinent to these entries. Though the current editors of *Larousse Gastronomique* have been keen to broaden beyond the encyclopedia's Francocentric roots, there are still plenty of ineffably French, offal-y recipes, such as the one for calf's head à l'occitane, which begins, "Cut half a well-soaked calf's head into 8 uniform pieces and cook in a white court-bouillon with the tongue."

Le Coze, Gilbert. Charismatic, pescatorially inclined chef from Brittany adored by Snobs for his boozy joie de vivre and his promulgation of the idea that fish cookery in America could be as good as France's. With his sister, Maguy, Le Coze opened Le Bernardin in New York in 1986, which quickly became a top-tier restaurant even as Le Coze himself preferred the company of the Fulton Fish Market's salty mongers to the city's swells. In his truncated life (he died of a heart attack in 1994, when he was just forty-nine), Le Coze was also quite the charmer, bedding (so she claims) *New York*'s "Insatiable Critic," Gael Greene, and shacking up with future club queen Amy Sacco.

Line-caught. Pet phrase of lyrical menu-writers, denoting a fish that has been caught in the old-fashioned rod-and-reel way, presumably by a small-time fisherman, rather than swooped up in a net with its entire school by a crew of unfeeling Russians on a huge, rusty trawler.

Live-fire grilling. Outdoor grilling over charcoal or wood; the only way to grill for Snobs, to whom fancy $5,000 gas grills with ignition buttons, griddles, and warming drawers are anathema, the wretched province of overprosperous sun-belt Republicans. Many Snobs concede, however, that the cylindrical "chimney starter" has been a worthwhile innovation.

Lomo. Cured Spanish pork tenderloin, usually served in thin slices as tapas. A beneficiary of the JAMON IBÉRICO–driven vogue for Spanish pig products, lomo has been posited by the aggressively food-forward as the "new prosciutto di parma." *Ed Levine arrived at our weekend house bearing a peach pie and the remnants of his jitney snack, sliced* lomo *and figs.*

Lucas, Dione. Petite Englishwoman and cookbook author notable for predating JULIA CHILD as a French-food authority in America, opening a cooking school in New York in the 1940s and hosting a syndicated TV program in the 1950s (old episodes of which were rebroadcast in the early days of the Food

Dione Lucas

Network). Though severe and bereft of warmth, Lucas knew how to teach, and Snobs (who pride themselves on knowing how to pronounce her first name: dee-OWN-ee) kick her props for popularizing the omelet at the modest restaurants she ran, the Egg Basket and the Gingerman.

Lusty. Stock adjective deployed by food writers to confer an air of unbridled peasant sensuality upon foodstuffs. *By the time I finished off the last of the* lusty *beef-cheek ravioli, Mario had reduced me to a quivering mess.*

THE FOOD SNOB
FILMOGRAPHY

Ten Films That All Food Snobs
Must Profess to Have Seen

Spartacus, directed by Stanley Kubrick (1960). For its conflation of mollusks and pansexual appetites in the bathhouse-flirtation scene ("My taste includes both snails and oysters") between Laurence Olivier and Tony Curtis.

Tom Jones, directed by Tony Richardson (1963). For Albert Finney's hammy, overwrought soup-slurping and lobster-tearing in the film's "erotically charged" feasting scene.

Tampopo, directed by Juzo Itami (1985). For being not much more than a bunch of lightweight comedy sketches for Japanese-noodle fetishists, but nevertheless becoming a major arthouse hit in the 1980s.

Heartburn, directed by Mike Nichols (1986). For supplying the opportunity to watch Meryl Streep "do" Nora Ephron as she cooked her way through her divorce from Carl Bernstein.

Babette's Feast, directed by Gabriel Axel (1987). For being the *locus classicus* of precious cinematic food porn, a beyond-faithful adaptation of Isak Dinesen's story of how a gray, churchy Danish village is brought to life by a haunted Frenchwoman who spends her inheritance on a blowout meal.

The Age of Innocence, directed by Martin Scorsese (1993). For the Scorsese spin, typically virtuosic, on a Whartonian Gilded Age goutfest: the Lovell Mingott family's orgy of terrapin soup (complete with a scene of footmen carting in the turtles live), canvasback duck, oysters, multiple desserts, etc.

Eat Drink Man Woman, directed by Ang Lee (1994). For basically being *Fiddler on the Roof* transposed to Taipei, with Master Chef Chu instead of Tevye the Milkman as the fretful father of many daughters, and busy Sunday banquet scenes instead of musical numbers.

Big Night, directed by Campbell Scott and Stanley Tucci (1996). For being the only authentically funny food movie, and for capturing the dynamics of a provincial Italian-American enclave without *Moonstruck*-style histrionics. And for Stanley Tucci and Tony Shalhoub's wordless omelet-making scene at the end.

Chocolat, directed by Lasse Hallström (2000). For combining all the classic elements of an unbearably twee food movie: an eccentric French village; adorably smudged tykes; a tightly wound cleric supposedly resistant to sensual pleasures; Johnny Depp doing a funny accent; and an enchantingly mysterious chocolatier who unshackles the villagers from their inhibitions. Who is played by Juliette Binoche. In a period blunt cut.

Spanglish, directed by James L. Brooks (2004). For attempting, no matter how misguidedly, to base an Adam Sandler character on Thomas Keller.

Macerate. Verb describing the process of softening or breaking down a food by soaking it in liquid, often a wine or liqueur that will also impart flavor. Long a common process among pastry chefs preparing fruit-based desserts, maceration is increasingly practiced by the sort of bartender who prefers to be called a mixologist. *The coup de grace of my saketinis is the addition of loquat plums* macerated *in Kirin Light.*

Marcona almonds. Addictive Spanish nuts that have recently emerged as an American status snack. Harvested from early-blooming trees along the Mediterranean coast, Marconas have a rich, macadamia-like MOUTHFEEL but a much fuller flavor than those premium Hawaiian nuts, which Food Snobs consider vulgar and whorish. Marconas are typically fried in SMALL BATCHES in vegetable oil and served dusted with FLEUR DE SEL.

Market menu. A bill of fare that changes on a regular basis, depending on what seasonal ingredients are locally available at a given moment, usually at a farmer's market in an urban setting. For the menu-reader, the term is a trigger to lapse into a reverie of a chef strolling through a narrow warren of bountiful stalls, wicker basket in hand, while purveyors stumble forth excitedly, offering him their choicest ingredients. In rare cases, like that of New York chef Wylie Dufresne, this fantasy is actually true.

Maytag Blue Cheese. Old-school American ARTI-SANAL cheese, produced in Iowa since 1941 by the same Maytags whose patriarch, F.L., started the appliance company of the same name. Way ahead of the curve, F.L.'s grandson, Fred II, who ran a dairy farm on the side, determined that the milk from his Holsteins could produce a veined, stinky cheese every bit as good as France's, and that the word *bleu* could therefore be authoritatively replaced by the word *blue*. Packaged attractively in blue-accented foil wrappers, Maytag's SMALL-BATCH cheeses are a popular name-drop on NEW AMERICAN menus.

McGee, Harold. Food-science god and author of the Snob must-read *On Food and Cooking: The Science and Lore of the Kitchen,* which was published in 1984 and revised in 2004; declared "the most important person alive writing about food" by Bill (*Heat*) Buford. McGee's friendly, conversational tone has engaged chefs and home cooks who want to understand the chemistry of foods and cooking (e.g., why kneading elongates gluten strands, why chili peppers are hot). Still, the unwieldiness and information overload of the volume scares off many casual cooks, for whom the book is the gastronomical equivalent of Stephen Hawking's unit-shifting but seldom read *A Brief History of Time*. The Snob com-

Harold McGee

munity couldn't believe its luck when McGee started blogging on his curiouscook.com site in 2006.

Meyer lemon. Small, soft-skinned citrus fruit of more orangey color and flavor (and higher price) than an everyday lemon; named after Frank Meyer, a Department of Agriculture employee who found the lemons growing in China and helped introduce them to the U.S. market in the early twentieth century. With their thin rinds, Meyer lemons are not good for making ZEST, but they are embraced by pastry chefs for the sweet-tart quality they impart to pies, soufflés, and sorbets, and by menu-writers for the opportunity they present to add another upmarket modifier to dessert descriptions.

Microplane. Registered trademark for a family of extremely sharp-edged graters whose holes aren't punched out of a sheet of metal but formed via a photochemical process in which points in the metal surface are dissolved, leaving clean edges that shred and ZEST beautifully and unraggedly. Produced for kitchen use only since the 1990s (by an Arkansas manufacturer that previously made parts for the printing industry and has now branched out into making foot files for exfoliating one's heels), the Microplane has quickly established itself as the Snob-standard grater. *Added some kick to the pumpkin soup with some ginger-root filings from the* Microplane.

Mineral flavor. Phrase used by Meat Snobs to describe the elusive steak-y, savory, *manly* quality of a cut of beef that is complemented by the creamy flavor and texture of the fat. *My porterhouse emerged from the Buenos Aires kitchen charred and sizzling, and the first bite yielded a dizzying blast of* mineral flavor *that you don't get from wimpy American beef.*

Mise en place. Fancy French term for doing all one's food prep before actually cooking—chopping, measuring, arranging, cleaning up, and so on. Especially Snobworthy when shortened to *meez* and used as a verb. *Honey, I've* meezed *everything for Julia's* supremes de volaille à blanc, *now all we need is for our guests to arrive.*

Molecular gastronomy. Techno-futurist approach to cookery that applies scientific manipulation—and elaborately silly utensils and serving implements—to the gastronomical experience. Coined as both a term and a discipline in the 1980s by the Hungarian-born, Oxford-based physicist and amateur cook Nicholas Kurti (who proudly concocted an inverted baked Alaska, with a frozen outer layer and hot interior) and the French chemist-foodie Hervé This, molecular gastronomy was taken up as a cause by lab-rat chefs in the nineties and aughts, most notably This's buddy Pierre Gagnaire in France, FERRAN ADRIÀ in Spain, HESTON BLUMENTHAL in England, and

Wylie Dufresne and Grant Achatz in America. *As off-putting as it may sound, the deconstructed "lumberjack breakfast" of mini-pancakes served on an octo-tined standing fork with Canadian-bacon "ketchup," atomized eggs, and crab syrup was a triumph of* molecular gastronomy.

Mouthfeel. Food- and wine-writer term that literally describes how an edible or potable substance feels in the mouth, but often carries a discomfiting erotic undercurrent. *Keller's signature pairing of oysters and tapioca has a slurpy, slippery* mouthfeel *that can't help but put one in the mood.*

Nestle, Marion. Leading American food scholar, renowned for her unintimidated takedown of evil Big Food, *Food Politics: How the Food Industry Influences Nutrition and Health,* and her stewardship of New York University's Department of Nutrition and Food Studies. Snobs pride themselves on knowing the correct pronunciation of her last name (*nessle,* not *nest-lee*).

New American. Ambiguous label used to describe cuisine prepared by American chefs who cook with indigenous ingredients but don't hew to traditional, French-based kitchen orthodoxies, and/or chefs who put modern twists on Olde American–style cookery, e.g., serving New England johnnycakes topped with Burgundy-braised short ribs. In increased vogue since the 1980s, the term usually evokes agreeable restaurants with house-made ketchup, farmhouse décor, and pots of fresh herbs on the table, but occasionally is used as cover for a flailing chef who has no idea of his identity.

Newtown Pippin. Homely, tart, green-skinned HEIRLOOM apple variety native to the Long Island section of New York State. An ideal apple for baking and cider-making, the Newtown Pippin is also upheld by righteous SLOW FOOD people as one of the historical gems that was nearly rendered extinct by the evil, Frankenfruit-favoring hybridiz-

Newtown Pippin

ers of agribusiness. *If you care about good fruit—if you're a feeling, compassionate human being—you'll join us in our efforts to help reestablish the* Newtown Pippin.

Niman Ranch. Marin County, California–based purveyor of all-natural, hormone- and antiobiotic-free beef, pork, and lamb products. Originally popular principally in Snob meccas like Chez Panisse and Union Square Café, Niman Ranch products are now finding their way onto, and conveying status upon, the menus of cheapie burger joints and the national burrito chain Chipotle. Founded in the 1970s by ex-schoolteacher Bill Niman (whose name, Snobs know, is pronounced NY-man, not NEE-man) and, oddly enough, the journalist and China expert Orville Schell, who has since left the company. *It looked like a dump, but the ratty old truck stop surprised us with sumptuous BLTs made with* Niman Ranch *bacon*.

Nouvelle cuisine. Painfully misunderstood upstart French food movement of the 1970s. As practiced by such chefs as Paul Bocuse, Roger Vergé, Michel Guérard, Georges Blanc, Louis Outhier, and the brothers Jean and Pierre Troisgros, nouvelle cuisine rejected the notion that high-end French cookery had to adhere to the precepts of ESCOFFIER, and placed a premium on "letting the ingredients taste like what they are," relying less on thick sauces and long cooking times. Snobs love to clear up the misperceptions that nouvelle chefs favored tiny portions and rejected cream-based sauces, noting that it was *flour*-based sauces that the nouvelle-ers shunned. (Only Guérard, who worked out of a spa resort, explicitly conceived a low-fat, dietetic menu, which he called *cuisine minceur*.) Though the nouvelle cuisine crew found kindred spirits in the Francophilic, fresh-foodist Californians of the early CHEZ PANISSE era, the term itself somehow lost its original meaning in the United States, and, by the 1980s, came to denote miniature portions of meat served on enormous plates with squeeze-bottle splatters of fruity sauce all over them.

Olney, Richard. Expatriate American food and wine writer (1927–1999) who, settling in France in the 1950s, earned a place alongside ELIZABETH DAVID as a Snob-revered expert on *cuisine bourgeoise,* the everyday fare prepared by dutifully food-reverent French home cooks. Though his tart, opinionated prose was not nearly as cuddly as David's, his recipes were far more precise and user-friendly. His *The French Menu Cookbook* (1970) and *Simple French Food* (1974) proved essential in the early seventies to Chez Panisse's culinary visionaries, ALICE WATERS and JEREMIAH TOWER, the latter of whom took up with Olney romantically for a time. *There's no better supper in late spring than a hunk of pain au levain and* Richard Olney'*s baked eggs with sorrel.*

Omakase. Immoderately priced Japanese tasting menu. Roughly translated as "trust in me," *omakase* usually involves a succession of small dishes devised by the chef as deliberate series of processions: from cool to hot, mild to assertive, raw to cooked. Often prepared and eaten right at a sushi bar, the *omakase* meal, with its triple-digit price tag, businessman demographic, and strange air of simultaneous intimacy and awkwardness between host and guest, is the closest gastronomical approximation of the escort-john experience.

Ortolan. Tiny, thumb-sized songbird of the bunting family, eaten whole by French stunt-diners, who regard it as a delicacy. According to centuries-old custom, the bird is captured, fattened with millet and oats, drowned in Armagnac, plucked, roasted, and devoured, bones and all, by a diner wearing a napkin over his head, the better to fully take in the bird's allegedly intoxicating aromas. Though the ortolan is now endangered in France, and therefore illegal to capture and eat, its bones are still masticated by thrill-seeking American expense-accounters with enough euros to bribe a chef, and by law-flouting French traditionalists; former president François Mitterrand ate one on his deathbed in 1996.

Oxo. Kitchen-equipment manufacturer famous for its Good Grips line of aesthetic, ergonomically friendly kitchen utensils, whose bulbous handles are made of a black, rubbery material called Santoprene. Authentically cook-friendly, Oxo Good Grips spoons, spatulas, and can-openers are vexing only because, given their bulk, they don't always fit in shallow kitchen drawers or countertop "utensil pitchers."

Palladin, Jean-Louis. Dead chef of madcap demeanor who put Washington, D.C., on the culinary map in the 1980s with his eponymous restaurant in the Watergate complex, Jean-Louis. Instantly identifiable thanks to his poodle hair, comedy mustache, and *Tootsie* eyeglasses, Palladin is lamented, like GILBERT LE COZE, as a chef-god who died too soon (in 2001, at fifty-five, after a debilitating battle with lung cancer) to fully reap the rewards of the celebrity-chef era. *That jerk owes everything he knows to* Palladin, *yet never mentions him in the acknowledgments.*

Jean-Louis Palladin

Panino. Toasted, pressed sandwich made from small slices of Italian ciabatta bread—or, increasingly, any old bread rendered crinkly and grill-marked by a press. Frequently misused in its plural form, *panini,* by non-Snobs, e.g., *Hon, do me a favor and grill me a Nutella* panini.

Panko. Shardy, flaky Japanese bread crumbs, used traditionally for fried foods like tempura, and, less traditionally, for non-Japanese dishes prepared by chefs smitten with the crumbs' airy, Rice Krispies–like crunch. Left undiscussed in most Snob exaltations of panko is that its crisp-keeping and nonsogging qualities come from the trans-fat-laden partially hydrogenated oils usually used in making the crumbs.

Peekytoe crab. Formerly undistinguished trash shellfish, astutely repurposed as a gourmet food by Rod Mitchell, the fishmonger whose Portland, Maine–based Browne Trading Company is best known in Snob circles as chef Daniel Boulud's seafood and caviar supplier. The peekytoe, a sand or rock crab that sometimes comes up in lobster traps, yields sweet, pinkish meat. The crab's name is a Mainer-dialect corruption of "pickèd toe," referring to the sharp, inverted tips of its claws. *And with the chef's compliments, here is a lagniappe of* peekytoe crab *with green apple slices.*

PEI mussels. Distinctively briny shellfish from Prince Edward Island in Canada, the island's second-most-famous export after *Anne of Green Gables.* With the possible exceptions of Olympia oysters (Pacific Northwest) and Nantucket bay scallops (Massachusetts), no other North American bivalve mollusk gets such play on fine-dining menus. *Chef Moonen got us off to a rollicking start with* PEI mussels *in a piquant, lemongrass-infused Thai broth.*

Plating. Professional-kitchen term, appropriated by Snobs, describing the meticulous process of arranging food appropriately and attractively on or in a serving vessel before it is delivered to the customer. *His architectural* plating *of the grilled lamb slices and roast yucca spears, complete with a moat of mango-colored* jus *and a forest of wilted tatsoi, was glorious to look at, but the flavors didn't mesh.*

Plugrá. Purportedly "European-style" butter manufactured by Keller's Creamery, the American dairy-products conglomerate that also owns the Borden, Breakstone's, and Hotel Bar companies. Made with a higher fat content than ordinary butter (*plus gras* is French for "fattier"), Plugrá, a favorite of chefs, delivers tenderer pastries and more velvety sauces—not to mention Atkins-approved arterial sclerosis.

Point, Fernand. Proudly rotund French chef (1897–1955) who, as the visionary behind La Pyramide, a restaurant in the old Roman settlement of Vienne, rejected the strictures of ESCOFFIER and, in his manifesto, *Ma Gastronomie,* encouraged French chefs to develop their own vocabulary, earning him the James Brown–ish sobriquet "the godfather of nouvelle cuisine." Frequently name-checked by such current godheads as THOMAS KELLER, ALAIN DUCASSE, and Paul Bocuse, the latter of whom actually trained under Point.

Fernand Point

Porchetta. Central Italian roasted-pig preparation, traditionally involving a whole boned pig stuffed with fresh herbs, fennel, garlic, and salt. Though customarily served on holidays in Umbria (where there are specialists known as *porchettaio*), porchetta has benefited in America from the recent rise in stature of pig meat and urban-barnyard restaurants with their own wood-burning ovens. Still, few U.S. chefs have embraced the *porchettaio* custom of stuffing the pig with its own offal.

Poulet de Bresse. Chicken native to the French town of Bourg-en-Bresse, reputed to be the most mind-alteringly flavorful fowl possible. So revered in France that it has been accorded its own AOC classification (the only chicken so honored), the Bresse, with its telltale shiny blue feet, was long considered a gastronomic experience one could enjoy only in eastern France, until some enterprising American and Canadian poultry breeders figured out a way to raise a similar bird in California. The American version, known as the blue foot chicken, crashed expensive menus in the early twenty-first century, taking its place alongside the Kobe steer and the Berskhire pig as a barnyard master race.

Pulses. Exasperatingly counterintuitive term for the edible seeds of legume plants, e.g., lentils, beans, and peas. (The word derives from the same Latin root as "pollen.") Primarily used by English ladies and vegetarian cookbook writers looking to liven up their prose. *This broad bean salad with mint and tomatoes is a must for anyone with a passion for* pulses.

Purslane. Low-spreading plant with fleshy, succulent, wedge-shaped leaves. Better known as a nuisance weed until FORAGERs and American-cuisine builder-uppers like Larry Forgione repositioned it as a salad green, beloved for its light, vaguely lemony flavor.

Purslane

FIVE ANNOYING
ZAGAT TICS

Why Food Snobs Consider
Zagat Survey Guidebooks Useful Only for
Addresses and Phone Numbers

Use of the word *eclectic* as a noun. E.g., "The 'multi-culti noshes' are 'always a gas' at this downtown eclectic."

Use of the word *yearling* to describe a restaurant in its second year. E.g., " 'The hype and fashionistas are gone' from this Market District yearling, but the wood-fired pizzas are 'to die for.' "

That touristy, overfloristed, super-expensive place with bad food that somehow gets high ratings across the board every year. And usually has lots of white stretch limos idling outside.

The Special Features section in the back includes categories for "People-Watching" and

"Senior Appeal." Not to mention "Singles Scenes" and "Trendy."

No one you know has ever been one of the surveyors. And why is the default voice of the surveyors that of a suburban ophthalmologist's wife?

Quark. Fresh, German-style curd cheese, increasingly popular on American menus and in ARTISANAL-skewing cheese shops. Pitched somewhere between ricotta and yogurt, quark can be spread on bread and eaten as is or used as an ingredient in desserts and heavy, Alfredo-type sauces. Frequently confused by Novice Snobs with *SPECK,* which, while German, is not a cheese but a ham. *We have one special tonight, an outstanding lavender* quark *cheesecake with candied figs.*

Quince. Astringent, apple-like fruit indigenous to the Mediterranean coast, edible only when cooked. Though traditionally used in jellies and pastes such as the Spanish *membrillo* (the burnt-orange, shivery glop served with Manchego cheese), quince is now being taken up by pastry chefs, the most perverse of Food Snob subcultures, as an ingredient in things like autumn fruit compote and tarte tatin.

Quinoa. Baffling fixture of chic menus (pronounced KEEN-wah) that, though it sounds like a Japanese management concept, is actually an ancient Incan grain-like substance whose popularity has been revived by vegan zealots and RAW FOOD–ists, who uphold it as an ideal protein and fiber source, and also by modern chefs, who put it on plates when they feel like serving an "interesting" starch instead of rice or couscous. Technically, though, quinoa is not a grain but the seed of a leafy plant related to chard.

Ranhofer, Charles. Elegant, fearsomely mustachioed French-born chef (1836–1899) who ran the kitchens of Delmonico's, New York's greatest nineteenth-century dining palace, on and off from 1862 until his death. Already etched into the Food Snob annals as America's first celebrity chef, his name familiar even to those outside of the gastronomic world (Charles Dickens wrote about him after sampling Ranhofer's food during an 1867 visit to the United States), Ranhofer posthumously won new renown in 1976, when JEREMIAH TOWER, looking to break free from the Francophile tendencies of Chez Panisse, found a recipe in Ranhofer's 1894 cookbook, *The Epicurean,* for cream of corn soup "à la Mendocino," after the Northern California town. Inspired by Ranhofer's surprising localist boosterism, Tower planned a menu for a "Northern California regional dinner," thereby putting the area on the map as a culinary region and a magnet for self-satisfied foodies.

Raw food. Bonkers, militant movement that uses a sensible premise—that lots of ingredients taste better and provide more nutrition in their uncooked state, and that the techniques of heatless food preparation are underexplored by American chefs—as a launch-pad for an absolutist argument that cooking is the enemy of life, because heating food above 118 degrees destroys not only nutrients but the enzymes that aid proper digestion, resulting in ulcers, arteriosclerosis, and other horrors. That most people willingly eat foods they know not to be 100-percent healthful in the pursuit of *pleasure*—the ultimate goal of cookery—seems utterly lost on ascetic raw-foodists, though it must be said that the movement's high priestess, the glowing, replicant-like Roxanne Klein (of Roxanne's to Go, the retail outlet of her now-shuttered Marin County restaurant), makes a good faux pad thai with coconut strands substituting for noodles.

Raw-milk cheese. Any cheese made with unpasteurized goat's, cow's, or sheep's milk. Raw-milk cheeses are vigorously championed by Cheese Snobs as superior, because the microorganisms within them allegedly bring a complexity of flavor to the finished product that pasteurized cheeses lack. *I don't care what my OB-GYN says about listeria, there's no way I can give up* raw-milk cheese *for my whole damned pregnancy.*

Razor clams. Edible bivalve Americana. Sweeter than a "regular" clam and attractively packaged in tubular, pearlescent shells, razors are especially revered by patriotic U.S. culinarians because a) they lend themselves well to the very American pastime of grilling, and b) because JAMES BEARD loved them. *We dug up* razor clams *at the dawn's low*

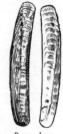

Razor clams

tide, dozens of 'em, anointed 'em with some lard-bait from Paw-Paw's tackle box, and ate 'em grilled over a firepit right in the sand—a true Oregonian's breakfast.

Reefer. Professional-kitchen shorthand for "refrigerator," employed to giggly effect by in-the-know Snobs.

Reichl, Ruth. Prodigiously maned gastro-sensualist and writer, known for a trilogy of memoirs—*Tender at the Bone, Comfort Me with Apples,* and *Garlic and Sapphires*—that chart her Zelig-like journey through various food-mad locales (Berkeley, Los Angeles, New York) as they experienced their signal moments in America's culinary coming of age. Though prone to onanistic, self-aggrandizing prose and batty flights of fancy—wearing unnecessarily elaborate disguises while visiting restaurants, frequently invoking her dead mother as a speaking character in reviews—Reichl has more than creditably served as the editor of *Gourmet* since 1999.

Roadfood. Landmark book-length roundup of cheap-eats spots across America, compiled by the Yale-educated kitsch enthusiasts Jane and Michael Stern. With its jes'-folks glorification of pit barbecue, griddle cookery, all-you-can-eat church suppers, and desserts so good they're even better as breakfasts (or so Jane Stern has a habit of insisting), *Roadfood* has struck a nerve since its original publication in

1977—blossoming into a cottage industry of updated editions, a Web site, a *Gourmet* column, and merchandise. Still, the Sterns' charming jollity is occasionally punctured by a class-warrior Reverse Snobbery that dictates that their greasy-spoon heroes are glorified at the expense of phony bourgie yuppie types, even though these are the people who make up their readership.

Romanesco. Broccoli-cauliflower hybrid with gorgeous, pale-green geometric florets. A quirky alternative to the cruciferous vegetables normally plopped on plates to give people their vitamins, romanesco is frequently confused by Novice Snobs with the sauce ROMESCO, which has nothing to do with it.

Romanesco

Rombauer, Irma. St. Louis housewife from well-to-do family who compiled the original version of *The Joy of Cooking* in 1931 to occupy her as she grieved over her husband's death by suicide. Adored by Snobs not so much for her catchall cavalcade of recipes but for her unmistakable voice and culinary nods to her German heritage, which, Snobs are fond of complaining, were watered down or eliminated completely in subsequent, putatively inferior versions of the cookbook (some of which were overseen by Rombauer's daughter, Marion Becker). *Don't give me any* *of these so-called "revisions" of* Joy; *I only cook with Scribner's facsimile of the 1931* Irma.

Romesco. Catalonian sauce rife with nuts, garlic, and tomatoes; northeastern Spain's analogue to pesto, typically used to dress seafood dishes. Frequently confused by Novice Snobs with the vegetable ROMANESCO, which has nothing to do with it.

Root, Waverly. Preciously named food historian (1903–1982) who cut his teeth as a Paris-based reporter for the *Chicago Tribune* in the 1920s, befriending that era's Lost Generation coterie of expat American bohemians and falling in love with French cuisine. Increasingly preoccupied with eating as well as possible, Root became the prototypical genially overstuffed overseas correspondent, setting the stage for *The New Yorker*'s A. J. Liebling (who, though a contemporary of Root's, settled in Paris later) and the *New York Times*'s R. W. "Johnny" Apple. Root's travelogue/culinary guide *The Food of France* (1958) was *the* essential text for American food tourists in the sixties.

FOOD SNOB GUILTY PLEASURES

Six Things That Food Snobs Like Even Though They're Not Supposed To

Jif peanut butter. Yes, it has sugar and hydrogenated oil in it, but corporate peanut butter (Skippy, too) simply tastes better than natural peanut butter, whose oil and solids separate no matter how much they're stirred, making some mouthfuls feel like an oil slick and others like tile grout.

Hot dogs. Snobs will demur and say that they only care for all-natural versions made without nitrites. Except they're lying.

Cheez Whiz. Smegmatic, but indispensable in authentic Philly cheesesteaks. Good on Triscuits, too, making it a Guilty Pleasure twofer.

Iron Chef. Sure, it has nothing to do with real cooking, but it is the most watchable thing on the Food Network.

French's French Fried Onions. Elevating Thanksgiving and Christmas green-bean casseroles for nigh on fifty years. "Seasonal produce" be damned.

Starbucks. "Eiewww, it's so corporate!" "Eiewww, their coffee tastes burned!" "Eiewww, all those losers on their laptops!" But it's still better than the corner deli or any other place at the airport.

Salamander. Squat, wide broiler beloved by professional chefs for its space efficiency and intense generation of heat, which cuts down on cooking times and is useful for finishing off the cooking of dishes that require browning and crisping. *We pulled the brûlées out of the oven and threw 'em in the* salamander *to caramelize the tops.*

Salsify. Confusingly named vegetable whose long, parsnip-like root is said to taste like an oyster when cooked but doesn't really. Correctly pronounced "SAL-si-fee," especially by Snobs who enjoy perplexing nouns that sound like verbs.

Salumi. Catchall Italian word for cured pork products, deployed by Snobs eager to demonstrate their grasp of the fact that they know the difference between salumi and salami—the latter of which, like pancetta and soppressata, is a *kind* of salumi.

Sand dab. Small flatfish unique to the Pacific Ocean. A favorite of JAMES BEARD, who in his native Oregon dusted them with flour and fried them whole, sand dabs are cherished especially by smug Californians who like to lord their region's culinary superiority over others (and who dismiss the larger Atlantic fish passed off as a sand dab as a variety of plaice).

Sand dab

Scharffen Berger. Deceptively German-sounding San Francisco chocolatier, named after cofounder and former winemaker John Scharffenberger. Virtually from the moment the company opened for business in 1997, Scharffen Berger chocolate (which has since been sold to the Hershey Company), produced by ARTISANAL methods, has been a favorite of both professional and home bakers. Available in 62, 70, and 99 percent versions (alluding to cacao-bean percentage)—otherwise known, in the terminology of non-Snobs, as semisweet, bittersweet, and unsweetened.

Seed Savers Exchange. Do-gooder nonprofit organization founded in 1975 to preserve HEIRLOOM plant varieties and endangered food crops. Based in Iowa, where its showcase Heritage Farm houses a seed-storage facility and an Amish-style visitor's center, the exchange affords gardeners the chance to cultivate such edible curios as the Golden Midget watermelon, the Giant Musselburgh leek, the Good Mother Stallard bean, and the Hinkelhatz pepper. *This year I'm gonna grow the Red Leprechaun lettuce from* Seed Savers *instead of the usual Giant Caesar stuff I get from Burpee.*

Shad roe. All-American delicacy with fleeting early-spring season, during the shad's run up the rivers from the salty sea. Though it tastes rather livery—indeed, a whole sac of it freshly taken from a fish more resembles a quivering human internal organ than a mound of caviar—shad roe is beloved by Heritage Snobs for having been eaten since colonial times in the Hudson River region, and because writer-angler John McPhee immortalized it (and its parent fish) in his book *The Founding Fish,* which features a recipe in which the roe is steamed inside a latticework of bacon.

Silpat. Reusable silicone cooking sheet that, when placed on a counter or in a baking sheet, provides an ideal nonstick surface on which to roll out dough or bake confections; favored by home bakers and professionals over parchment paper, which, though more traditionalist, clings maddeningly to everything. *Ever since I switched over to* Silpats, *my tuiles are more beautiful than ever.*

Silver Spoon, The. Modishly chic Italian cookbook, regarded since its original publication in 1950, under the aegis of the design and architecture magazine *Domi,* as the definitive compilation of Italy's cookery (which actually varies dramatically in style and ingredients from region to region, as any Snob will remind you). Finally issued in the English language in 2006 (at a whopping 1,200-plus pages and $40 a pop), *The Silver Spoon*'s concise, authorless recipes are now easily executable in American kitchens, though

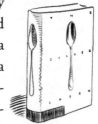

The Silver Spoon

Food Snobs like to insist that the Italian-language original is superior.

Single-origin. Modifier embraced in recent years by the high-end coffee and chocolate trades, denoting products made from beans that come from a specific geographic region, and, in some cases, from a specific plantation or patch of land. The allure of a single-origin coffee or hunk of chocolate is that it is supposed to offer a flavor experience unique to the land from whence it came, much in the way that an unblended wine is said to exude the essence of its terroir. *'Kay, next in our tasting is a single-origin 70 percent cacao chocolate from Sur del Lago in Venezuela—very masculine, very big, heavy molasses body, very typical of the region.*

Slider. Miniature hamburger originally popular at the low-rent White Castle chain, traditionally eaten in great quantities. Lately repopularized as a *ROAD-FOOD*-style binge snack for slumming Snobs, or, at certain fine-dining restaurants, as a bit of postmodern menu whimsy. *We clinked our beer bottles and washed down a dozen bison* sliders *served on brioche buns with cornichons.*

Slow Food. Dogmatic international movement with roots in Italy, devoted to the preservation of ARTISANAL food- and winemaking methods, and to environmental sensitivity in the cultivation of food crops. Local chapters of the movement—known, in the organization's Marxism-redolent vernacular, as convivia—organize events like cheese and SALUMI tastings while also functioning as advocacy groups for the preservation of such endangered food species as the Sheepnose pimento (an HEIRLOOM chili from Ohio) and the American Buff goose.

Small-batch. Adjective describing any ARTISANAL food product handcrafted in limited amounts. Usually deployed to suggest a martyrish devotion to ancient, toilsome production methods that yield a delicious, expensive edible (or bourbon whiskey). *Our* small-batch *bonbons are painstakingly crafted from the finest ingredients, including hand-harvested, fair-trade, demerara sugar from Mauritius.*

Soltner, André. French-born, New York–based chef, upheld by disparagers of the celebrity-chef phenomenon as the idealized one-stove, "*Le restaurant, c'est moi*" restaurateur of integrity whose type thrived before Wolfgang and Emeril came along and ruined everything. Presiding for thirty-four years over Lutèce, a restaurant rated in the 1970s as New York's finest, Soltner lived above the shop with his wife and shuttered it whenever he himself wasn't cooking. *Sometimes I find myself shuttling from the TV studio in L.A. to my new Vegas pan-Asian place and I* *think, "Shit, what's become of me? I started out think-ing I wanted to be Soltner."*

Sontheimer, Carl. MIT-trained engineer and com-pulsive tinkerer (1914–1998) whose love of cooking and eating resulted, after a prosperous career in elec-tronics, in a second act as the inventor of the Cuisi-nart food processor (which was actually a licensed, modified version of an industrial blender he found in France, Le Magimix). Though perceived as a dubious fad gadget upon its introduction in the early 1970s, the Cuisinart took off when the media-savvy Sont-heimer demo'd his gizmo for JULIA CHILD and JAMES BEARD, who pronounced it nothing less than a seismic development in the annals of home cookery. Thus did Cuisinarts become the coveted objects of elbows-out department-store wrangles in the mid-1970s, and did Sontheimer come to enjoy an odd sort of kitchen-implement celebrity not repeated until George Fore-man came along.

Carl Sontheimer

Soulé, Henri. Stout, imperious, penguin-like French-man who parlayed his stint as the overseer of France's dining facility at the 1939–40 World's Fair in Queens, New York, into a career as America's fore-most haughty French restaurateur. From 1941 until his death in 1966, Soulé presided over Le Pavillon, the grandest of New York's haute-snoot society dining palaces, whose alumni would go on to start La Caravelle, La Côte Basque, and most of the other "Le" and "La" restaurants of Manhattan's shiny mid-century. Flagrantly lookist and classist, Soulé introduced Americans to the idea of status tables (which he called "the Royale") and a "Siberia" for the ugly and less moneyed.

Soup dumplings. Bulging, pouch-like, Shanghai-style dumplings filled with hot broth in addition to the usual nubbin of ground pork (or other meat). Eaten with a soup spoon, to catch the leakage that gushes forth from the dumpling when its skin is broken by the diner's teeth, the soup dumpling rose to prominence in the 1990s, its slurpy, sensual qualities ideal for RUTH REICHL's heyday at the *New York Times*.

Sous-vide. French culinary term for Cryovacking, the process of vacuum-packing a food in plastic. Hailed by FERRAN ADRIÀ acolytes as a revolutionary technology that allows them to change the texture of foods (resulting in, say, watermelon slices with the consistency of beef jerky) and to keep meats and fish flavorful and juicy as they slow-cook in hot liquid, *sous-vide* technology has been less impressive to health officials, who argue that the food inside the bags often doesn't reach a temperature sufficiently hot to kill harmful bacteria.

Southern Foodways Alliance. Folksy food society devoted to preserving the cooking, food writing, and tumid-gothic atmosphere of the kitchens of the American south. As its early-REM-album-title-like name implies, the Alliance is altogether more friendly and laid-back than the similarly missioned SLOW FOOD movement, devoting itself to such charmingly breezy undertakings as a Pimento Cheese Competition and an oral history of Papa KayJoe's Bar-B-Que in Centerville, Tennessee.

Speck. Smoked, dry-cured boneless ham indigenous to the Italian Alps, where the cultural influence is more German than Italian. The abrupt, unsensual nature of the word *speck*—which simply means bacon in German—is often confusing to Novice Snobs, who mistake the pork product for such unrelated foodstuffs as spelt, the southern European grain, or QUARK, the German curd cheese. In reality, *speck* is often sliced and served with figs like a fine prosciutto or chopped and added to a carbonara sauce like bacon.

Stage. French verb (pronounced *stahj*) that has passed into American-kitchen parlance, describing the act of serving a short, unpaid apprenticeship at a restaurant—in typical usage, a prestigious one overseas—in order to learn at the feet of a master. *I did nothing but trim haricots verts, but man,* staging *for Guérard in Eugénie-les-Bains changed my life.* Sometimes used in noun form, *stagiaire*, e.g., *I was Gordon Ramsay's stagiaire-bitch for a week at Aubergine in the midnineties, and he was even worse then.*

Stone fruit. The large-pitted fruits of the *prunus* genus, among them peaches, plums, nectarines, apricots, and cherries; exalted by Fruit Snobs for their sensual juiciness and delicacy as compared to hardier fruits like apples and pears. The received Snob wisdom is that most Americans have never properly experienced stone fruits in their ideal ungassed, unshipped, unhybridized state, in which they are so succulent and dribbly that eating them qualifies as an erotic experience. *In the tumid fullness of the July night, we feasted on just-picked white peaches, the most luscious of* stone fruits, *their effluvia streaming down our heaving, perspiring chests.*

Stone fruit

Straus Family Creamery. Long-running, standard-bearing dairy farm in Northern California, devoted to organic production and SUSTAINABLE AGRICULTURE long before smug boomers were calling attention to such things. Launched in 1941 by Bill and Ellen Straus and twenty-three cows, Straus Family Creamery sells its milk in thick glass bottles and offers butterfat-rich European-style butter that California Snobs prefer over PLUGRÁ.

Sub-Zero/Wolf. High-end kitchen-appliance behemoth formed in 2000 when the Sub-Zero Freezer Company, the nation's leading manufacturer of heavy-doored, fancy-shmancy refrigerators, acquired Wolf Appliance, a longtime manufacturer of professional cooking ranges. Wolf, which in recent years has adapted its products for home use, edges out the equally formidable Viking range as the Snob's choice only because Vikings were developed specifically for home cooks, with no restaurant pedigree. (For similar reasons, some refrigeration Snobs prefer professional-grade Traulsen REEFERS to Sub-Zeros.) The truly hardcore gas-range Snob might also opt for the even more scarily industrial Vulcan and GARLAND ranges.

Sunchoke. Lyrical yet confusing alternative name for the already confusingly named Jerusalem artichoke, a starchy North American tuber grown for its bulbous root. In fairness, the sunchoke is horticulturally related to the sunflower and possessed of a slightly artichoke-like FLAVOR PROFILE. *Our degustation meal started out with little demitasse cups of sunchoke purée dotted with house-made crème fraîche.*

Super-Rica Taqueria, La. Tatty, inexpensive taqueria in Santa Barbara, California, that achieved Food Snob renown when JULIA CHILD, who retired to neighboring Montecito in her final years, became a regular. Though the torn-canvas roof and lines out the door suggest an enervating exercise in underwhelming reverse chic, the tacos—made with thick, homemade corn tortillas, some featuring such offbeat ingredients as stewed zucchini—are actually good.

Sustainable agriculture. Farming philosophy that advocates producing food in an ecologically considerate and humane manner. An all-encompassing ethos, sustainable agriculture involves both a moral dimension (the fair and equitable treatment of farm workers, ensuring that farming endures as a viable profession) and a rigorous commitment to self-sufficiency through the incorporation of natural biological cycles and controls—e.g., letting fields lie fallow so their soil can "recover" from a previous growing season, and rotating animals and crops from one parcel of land to the next so that the chickens manicure the pastureland vacated by the cows, and the strawberries blossom through the soil fertilized by the chickens, etc. Despite its inherently upbeat mission, sustainable agriculture has become a rallying cry for dour Issue Snobs looking for something to be shrill and strident about. *Goddamnit, we have got to get our school districts to buy milk from dairy co-ops that support* sustainable agriculture*!*

Taste memory. Evocative phrase, coined by JAMES BEARD in his 1964 memoir, *Delights and Prejudices,* to describe the ability to recall in intense detail a flavor experience from the past, often in order to compare it to one currently being experienced. *Jim's taste memory was such that I could put a ramekin full of butter in front of him, he'd take a generous lick of it from his finger, and say "Definitely Shawano County, Wisconsin—too nutty to be Oconto County."*

Tea sommelier. Inessential but increasingly existent FRONT OF THE HOUSE employee, available in more precious restaurants to guide the diner through a lengthy selection of teas and TISANEs, suggest tea pairings with food, and even offer tea FLIGHTs. An American named James Labe claims to have been the first tea sommelier, inaugurating that position in 1998 at the W New York Hotel.

Tisane. Newly modish and more factually accurate term (pronounced tee-ZAHN) for what has long been called herbal tea. As Tea Snobs know, actual tea, whether green, yellow, white, black, or oolong, must be made with leaves from some variety of *Camellia sinensis,* the tea plant. A tisane, by contrast, can be made from herbs, dried flowers, seeds, roots, and leaves of other plants; steeped in hot water, these ingredients produce what is technically an infusion, not a cup of tea. *Our enlightened blenders have foraged the* mountains and the forests of faraway lands to bring you the most transcendent and healing tisanes.

-top. Restaurant-lingo suffix denoting the number of guests that can be accommodated at a specific table, e.g., a two-*top* for two diners, a four-*top* for four diners. Used by Snobs to sound knowing and insidery. *I'll call Wolf on his private line and see if he can get us a four-*top *at Spago.*

Tower, Jeremiah. Merchant-Ivory handsome and omnisexual sophisticate-libertine who improbably landed the job of chef at Chez Panisse in 1973, elevating its cuisine from humble bistro fare to FERNAND POINT–inspired levels of sophistication, and establishing himself as the great rival/complement to ALICE WATERS in the Food Snob's favorite soap opera. Frequently photographed in black tie, raising a Champagne flute. After finally leaving Chez Panisse in 1978 (and enjoying a brief affair with RICHARD OLNEY), Tower forsook the Birkenstock ripeness of Berkeley for San Francisco society, opening the glamorous brasserie Stars, which flourished as the definitive non-L.A. California restaurant of the 1980s. Has since lived an itinerant life as a consultant, tart memoirist, newspaper columnist, puncturer of Panisse mythology, and snorkeler.

Jeremiah Tower

Turbot. North Atlantic flatfish with pronunciation issues. A white-fleshed finfish of mild flavor, turbot is held in such high esteem in classic French cookery that it has been afforded its own eponymous, species-specific cooking vessel, the *turbotière*. Still, ordering the fish at a restaurant is a confounding, often embarrassing experience for Americans, because the French, who usually pronounce the syllable *ot* as "oh" if it's at the end of a word, perversely pronounce the word "TER-bit."

Two ways. Var. *three ways* or *four ways*. Whimsical presentation of a specific food, usually a meat or fish course, presented in two (or more) preparations on the same plate, e.g., duck presented on one side as a confit and on the other side as a grilled breast fanned out under apricot COULIS. *I can never pass up Jean-Georges's lobster* four ways.

Umami. Elusive "fifth taste" that the tongue's receptors experience in addition to the traditional, more understandable tastes: sweet, sour, salty, and bitter. Umami was first posited as a taste in 1908 by Dr. Kikunae Ikeda of Tokyo Imperial University as he tried to nail down the appeal of kombu, an edible seaweed popular in Japan. The word *umami,* while not directly translatable into English, is often described as "savoriness," "richness," or "deliciousness," and this quality is attributed to the presence in foods of glutamates, amino acids commonly found in meats and cheese. It was Ikeda's work that led to the manufacture and popularity in Asia of monosodium glutamate (MSG), an additive that helps foods up their umami quotient. Though Food Snobs regard MSG with contempt, they are fascinated with the concept of umami. Unlike the other four tastes, umami has its own international organization, the Umami Information Center, which sponsors an annual Umami Symposium.

Verjus. Medieval vinegar variant, made from the nonfermented juice of unripe grapes, that has insinuated its way back onto menus, thanks to the efforts of ARTISANAL producers and chefs who like to use it as an "interesting" substitute for lemon juice. *We cleansed our palates with a pleasingly sweet-tart strawberry*-verjus *granita.*

Wagyu. Marketing term for richly marbled beef that comes from the same cattle as Kobe beef but costs somewhat less. Though both Kobe and Wagyu beef come from the Wagyu bull (the word *wagyu* simply means "Japanese cattle"), Kobe beef must come from cattle actually raised in Kobe, in accordance with severe, AOC-like production strictures, whereas Wagyu beef can come from cattle raised in the United States. Snobs, though they consider certified Kobe beef a vulgar folly for expense-account schmucks, are more kindly disposed toward Wagyu and are keen to flaunt their knowledge that the beef is best served Japanese-style—sliced thinly and either quickly seared or served raw, sashimi-style—rather than cooked as a slab in the broiler.

Walk-in. Refrigerated closet that serves as a restaurant's major cold-storage area. Because a walk-in must maintain a temperature no higher than 41°F, it is imperative that its door not be kept open too long—a source of major tension and histrionic screaming among amped-up kitchen staff during busy periods. *Get the fuck out of the* walk-in *before my goat's milk goes to shit!*

Waters, Alice. Former student activist and schoolteacher who founded Chez Panisse, the legendary Berkeley, California, bistro, in 1971, thereby launching California cuisine, the Snob mantra of

"fresh, local, seasonal ingredients," the desire/need for FORAGERs, and the general liberal-humanist tenor of the contemporary American food world. Fond of wearing cloche hats. Though undeniably a doer of good works, having founded a program that encourages schoolchildren to eat better and grow their own food, Waters has rather ickily embraced the latter-day food world's deification of her, reveling in the sort of cowed testimonials that intimidated flunkies offer up to Mob bosses.

Alice Waters

Waxman, Jonathan. Bearded boomer chef responsible for the "California cuisine" concept's metastasization to the East Coast. Forsaking his prestigious job at Michael's in Santa Monica, Waxman moved to New York and in 1984 opened Jams, which introduced cold-weather-climate people to mesquite-grilled chicken, open kitchens, and minimalist décor. A notorious "party chef" who drove a Ferrari for a time, Waxman overextended himself and flamed out at decade's end, but has since reemerged as an affable, humbled elder statesman and mentor figure, the Obi-Wan of professional cooking.

Well-edited. Voguish restaurant-critic adjective used to describe a thoughtfully brief bill of fare (e.g., a wine list or selection of entrees) at a bistro, usually of the tiny, charmingly rusticated variety. *We finished the last of the Condrieu with some pungent Pont l'Evêque from the frommagier-owner's well-edited cheese list.*

White honey. Labor-intensive, super-select organic raw honey from Hawaii, extracted from a single grove of flower-bearing kiawe trees on the state's big island. Pearlescent of appearance and buttery of texture, white honey has emerged as a luxe breakfast condiment thanks to the astute marketing of one bearded man, Richard Spiegel, a hippie lawyer turned back-to-the-lander who took up Hawaiian beekeeping in the 1970s. *I blended some* white honey *into my filbert butter and the result was positively ambrosial.*

Yuzu. Japanese citrus fruit prized for its highly aromatic rind. Traditionally used in dipping sauces for dumplings and spring rolls, yuzu is now being abused willy-nilly by Western chefs in their fusion experiments—though the fruit lost some of its Snob cachet when it became an ingredient in an aromatherapy body wash for sale on QVC.

Zest. The colored, aromatic outer layer of the peel of a citrus fruit, used in tiny shavings as a flavoring agent. Because of its cheery household-product ring (there is a deodorant soap called Zest and a variety of commercially manufactured lemon-zest powders), Novice Snobs sometimes mistakenly believe that zest is an odious supermarket product rather than a natural ingredient, and are surprised to find it in the recipes of ALICE WATERS. *Feeling frisky, I pepped up the Thanksgiving cranberry sauce with tangerine* zest.

Zest

Zingerman's. Funky gourmet-foods emporium in Ann Arbor, Michigan, that began its life in 1982 as a boomerized Jewish deli but has since morphed into a lifestyle arbiter for midwestern alterna-folks. Beloved for its ARTISANAL and traditional goods, its exuberant, stonerish sense of graphic design, and the steadfast refusal of its rumpled, Ben & Jerry–ish founders, Ari Weinzweig and Paul Saginaw, to open new locations in other cities, Zingerman's has thrived by expanding into an interrelated chain of local businesses, including Zingerman's Bakehouse, Zingerman's Creamery, Zingerman's Roadhouse (a restaurant), Zingerman's Mail Order, and even an enlightened business-management school, ZingTrain. *Got this awesome Sicilian fig jam at* Zingerman's; *Ari is a frickin' food-finding genius.*

About the Authors

DAVID KAMP has been a writer and editor for *Vanity Fair* and *GQ* for over a decade and began his career at *Spy* magazine. He lives in New York City.

MARION ROSENFELD, a writer and producer, has spent her entire career in media, much of it food-related. She was born, raised, and still lives in Greenwich Village with her husband, Thomas, and daughter, Theadora.

About the Illustrator

ROSS MACDONALD's illustrations have appeared in many publications, from *The New Yorker* and *Vanity Fair* to *Rolling Stone* and the *Wall Street Journal.* Two of his children's books, *Another Perfect Day* and *Achoo! Bang! Crash! The Noisy Alphabet,* have won *Publishers Weekly* Best Books of the Year for their categories. MacDonald lives in Connecticut with his wife, two children, four cats, two dogs, and a large collection of nineteenth-century type and printing equipment.

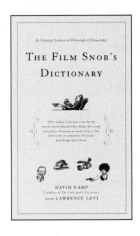